KETO MEAL PREP
FOR BEGINNERS

Table of Contents

INTRODUCTION 1

CHAPTER ONE: KETO MEAL
PREPARATION 4

   1.   SESAME BROILED CHICKEN 15

   2.   GREEK EGG BAKE.................................... 18

   3.   TURMERIC SCRAMBLED EGG 20

   4.   CAULIFLOWER HASH BROWNS 22

   5.   BLUEBERRY PANCAKE BITES 24

   6.   KETO BAGELS 26

   7.   LOW-CARB BREAKFAST PIZZA 29

   8.   KETO BACON SAUSAGE MEATBALLS........ 31

   9.   CREAM CHEESE & SALAMI KETO
       PINWHEELS 33

  10.   CHEESEBURGER LETTUCE WRAPS............ 35

  11.   SESAME SALMON WITH BABY
       BOK CHOY AND MUSHROOMS 37

  12.   BACON, CHICKEN & TOMATO STUFFED
       AVOCADO.. 39

13. KETO CHICKEN ENCHILADA BOWL............ 41

14. AVOCADO TUNA SALAD RECIPE................ 43

15. SHEET PAN CHICKEN FAJITAS.................... 45

16. SPICY MUSTARD THYME CHICKEN &
     COCONUT ROASTED BRUSSELS SPROUTS. 47

17. FATHEAD PIZZA CRUST RECIPE
     (LOW-CARB KETO PIZZA) 49

18. KETO LASAGNA WITH ZUCCHINI
     NOODLES... 52

19. ONE-PAN LEMON CHICKEN WITH
     ASPARAGUS 54

20 . CHEESY BACON-STUFFED MINI PEPPERS.. 58

21. STEAK BITES 60

22. KETO AVOCADO BROWNIES 62

23. COCONUT OIL FAT BOMBS 64

24. KETO BREAD.. 66

25. AVOCADO DEVILED EGGS RECIPE —
     THE IDEAL KETO SNACK 68

26. CHOCOLATE FAT BOMBS RECIPE 70

27. CAULIFLOWER-CRUSTED GRILLED
     CHEESE SANDWICHES 72

28. CHICKEN PAD THAI.................... 75

29. CINNAMON BUTTER FAT BOMBS 78

30. COCONUT OIL MAYONNAISE.................... 80

31. CREAMY CAULIFLOWER MASH AND
KETO GRAVY.................... 82

32. CRUSTLESS SPINACH QUICHE RECIPE 84

33. SIMPLE PALEO CHICKEN CURRY RECIPE.... 86

34. CAULIFLOWER MAC AND CHEESE............. 88

35. JALAPENO CHEDDAR BURGERS
(TURKEY OR BEEF).................... 90

36. ONION SOUP.................... 93

37. BABA GANOUSH.................... 95

38. PIZZA GRILLED CHICKEN.................... 97

39. BURGER COOK MUSHROOOM............... 100

40. EASY CHOCOLATE MOUSSE 102

41. LOW-CARB TACOS.................... 104

42. ALFREDO RECIPE 107

43. LOW-CARB BLUEBERRY MUFFINS........... 109

44. KETO BEEF WITH BROCCOLI.................... 112

45. EASY CROCKPOT CHICKEN STEW 115

46. KETO OATMEAL.................................... 117

47. LEMON THYME CHICKEN 121

48. KETO PANCAKES.................................. 123

49. KETO CHOCOLATE CHIA PUDDING 124

50. CHEESY GARLIC CREAMED SPINACH....... 126

51. CHICKEN IN WHITE SAUCE 128

52. GUILTLESS GARLIC PARMESAN WINGS... 130

53. Eggplant Rollatini Recipe 132

54. KETO SMOOTHIE RECIPE WITH AVOCADO, CHIA SEEDS & CACAO........... 134

55. LOW-CARB CAULIFLOWER POT PIES....... 136

56. JALAPENO POPPERS.............................. 139

57. KETO LOW-CARB GRANOLA CEREAL....... 141

58. KETO ZUCCHINI BREAD WITH WALNUTS.. 144

59. KETO WALNUT BREAD 146

60. LOW-CARB TORTILLA CHIPS................... 148

61. PUMPKIN SPICE KETO FAT BOMB RECIPE 150

62. EASY CHEESY ZUCCHINI GRATIN............ 151

63. KETO SNACKS 153

64. BLACKBERRY-NUT FAT BOMBS 155

65. BUFFALO KETO CHICKEN TENDERS 157

66. COCONUT KETO MILK 159

67. KETO CHEESE MEATBALLS 161

68. COCONUT BOOSTERS RECIPE.................. 163

69. BAKED MEATBALLS RECIPE 164

70. GOAT CHEESE & ARTICHOKE DIP
     RECIPE 166

71. LOW-CARB INDIAN SAMOSAS................. 168

72. CHOCOLATE AVOCADO PUDDING 172

73. LOADED HASSELBACK ZUCCHINI............. 173

74. GUILTLESS GARLIC PARMESAN WINGS... 176

75. EGGPLANT ROLLATINI RECIPE................. 178

76. MEATBALLS 180

HOW TO STORE FOOD SAFELY AND PREVENT
FOODBORNE ILLNESSES 183

CONCLUSION.. 188

INTRODUCTION

When the average person eats a meal rich in carbs, their body takes those carbs and converts them into glucose for fuel. Glucose is the body's main source of fuel when carbs are present in the body; on a Keto diet, there are very low if any at all carbs consumed, which forces the body to utilize other forms of energy to keep it functioning properly. This is where healthy fats come into play; with the absence of carbs, the liver takes fatty acids in the body and converts them into ketone bodies.

The ketogenic diet, or keto, is a diet that consists of very low carbs and high fat. That may sound too good to be true for many. Well, on this diet, this is a great day of eating and you can follow the rules perfectly with that meal plan.

A keto diet causes ketone bodies to be produced by the liver, and shifts the body's metabolism away from glucose in favor of fat-burning. A ketogenic diet restricts carbohydrates below a certain level (generally 100 per day). The ultimate determinant of whether a diet is ketogenic or not is the presence or absence of carbohydrates. Protein and fat intake vary. Contrary to popular belief, eating fat is not what causes ketosis. In the past, starvation diets were used often to induce ketosis

A lack of carbohydrates or presence of them ultimately determines if the diet is ketogenic.

In most eating plans, the body runs on a mixture of protein, fats, and carbohydrates. When carbohydrates are severely restricted and glycogen storage (glucose in muscle and liver) is depleted, the body begins to utilize other means to provide energy. FFA (free fatty acids) can be used to provide energy, but the brain and nervous system are unable to use FFA's. Although the brain can use ketone bodies for energy.

Ketone bodies are by products of incomplete FFA breakdown in the liver. Once they begin to accumulate fast and reach a certain level, they are released, accumulated in the bloodstream, and cause a state called ketosis. As this occurs, there is a decrease in glucose production and utilization. There is also less reliance on protein to meet energy requirements by the body. Ketogenic diets are often referred to as protein sparing, as they help to spare LBM while dropping body fat.

In regards to ketogenic diets, there are two primary hormones- insulin, glucagon that need to be considered. Insulin can be described as a storage hormone as its job is to take nutrients out of the bloodstream and carry them to target tissues. Insulin carries glucose from the blood to the liver and muscles, and it carries FFA from the blood into adipose tissue (stored fat triglyceride). On the other hand, glucagon breaks down glycogen stores (especially in the liver) and releases them into the blood.

When carbs are restricted or removed, insulin levels drop while glucagon levels rise. This causes an enhanced FFA release from fat cells, and increased FFA burning in the liver. This accelerated burning of FFA in the liver is what leads to ketosis. There are a number of other hormones involved with this process as well.

CHAPTER ONE:
KETO MEAL PREPARATION

Obesity rates have skyrocketed; the incidence of diabetes has also increased, the main reason being that people's diets consist mainly of carbohydrates and fats, and the two don't mix well together; but protein and fats do mix well together. Watching your intake of carbohydrates is very important for weight loss. Low-carb diets or diets that teach food combining are very effective in weight loss. Ok, now for the myths.

The truth is that the father of low-carb, high-protein dates back to 1863, William Banting of England, who wrote a little booklet titled "Letter on Corpulence Addressed to the Public", William Banting is considered the father of low-carbohydrate dieting. He proved this over years, helping people lose weight without any side-effects.

The myth says that a low-carb, high-protein, and high-fat diet raises cholesterol; the truth is it actually lowers cholesterol.For one year, researchers at the Veterans Affairs Medical Center in Philadelphia followed 132 obese adults randomized into two groups. One restricted carbohydrate intake to less than 30 grams per day (low-carbohydrate diet); the other restricted caloric intake by 500 calories, with 30% of calories from fat (conventional diet).83% percent of the study group had diabetes or other risk factors for heart disease.

In the low-carb group, triglyceride levels decreased more and HDL ('good') cholesterol levels decreased less than in the low-fat group (high levels of triglycerides, a fat in the blood, are associated with heart disease). People with diabetes on the low-carb diet had a better control of blood sugar.

The low-carbohydrate group had more beneficial changes in triglyceride levels and HDL cholesterol levels than the low-fat diet group; the low-carb diet group also contained vitamins and other nutritional supplements.

Another myth says that a low-carb diet will raise your blood pressure; the truth is, with lower LDL levels and VLDL levels, blood pressure levels drop.

If people have high blood pressure and a weight problem, a low-carbohydrate diet might be a better option than a weight-loss medication.

Another myth says that you need carbohydrates or glucose for brain function; the truth is if you are on a hardcore low-carb, high-protein diet, where carbohydrates are non-existent, you are on what is called a Ketogenic Diet. When on such a strict diet, your body produces ketones in the absence of carbohydrates, then converts the ketones into a form of glucose that enables proper brain function.

Will I gain all my weight back if I stop my low-carb diet ?. That is totally false, it does not matter what diet you choose, if you are successful in your weight loss and then stop your diet, 9 out of 10 times you revert back to your old eating habits, and start eating junk and over-indulge, then of course you gain the weight back.

-Another myth: eating protein makes you fat. This is totally false; protein actually raises your calorie-burning metabolism by as much as 30% over carbohydrates. When proteins are consumed, your body must digest and break them down into amino acids, this takes energy and plenty of it, this actually helps you lose weight; not gain it.

Another myth: high-protein diets include fats, and fats are bad for me. Fats in the absence of carbohydrates burn more efficiently, and do not clog your arteries. As the studies show LDL's (low density lipoproteins) which are the artery cloggers, are lowered. The HDL's, which are the good carbohydrates, are raised even though your fat intake is increased, that, as mentioned above is attributed to low-carb intake. Carbs and fat don't mix, your body cannot efficiently break them down together, your liver is over-burdened and ends up converting the carbohydrates into fat, unless of course you are exercising like crazy.

Anotyher myth states: I will not have any energy with the low-carb diet. This is totally false, unless you are a marathon runner or bodybuilder. When you consume small amounts of carbohydrates, your body needs another source of energy; when glycogen levels are gone, your body starts using fat for energy and combustion. If you are extremely active, then it will take about 2-3 weeks, after that, your body is acclimated to your new eating habits and adjusts, energizing you as before. If you are involved in a endurance sport, then of course you need extra carbs to be competitive. If you are an athlete or work-out extensively, then you probably would not be dieting anyway, and a low-carb high-protein is a mute point.

Here are the most common myths associated to the low-carb diet plan.

1. It has been said that the low-carb diet will reduce the amount of calcium in your body. This couldn't be farther from the truth, as since the low-carb diet is rich in protein, this, in fact actually prevents calcium from entering your urine.

2. They say the low-carb diet plan will damage one's kidneys. Not unless one already has a kidney defect, because with the low-carb diet, though rich in protein, this is not what the entire meal is made of. Once on a low-carb diet, one still must observe the balancing of the meals consumed. It has been said that some doctors actually recommend a low-carb diet for some of their patients in order to treat kidney problems.

3. Moving from the kidneys, there's also this myth that while on a low-carb diet, you're dicing with heart disease. On the contrary, it's

a fact that a low-carb diet plan actually reduces the risk of having heart disease. It has also been proven that even foods containing lots of animal fat and proteins do not constitute risk for heart disease.

4. There is no fibre present in the low-carb diet. The low carb diet is, on the contrary, full of fibre, and research also shows that the presence of this fibre actually lessens the effect and the amount of carbohydrates in one's body. Which makes the low-carb diet a very pragmatic diet plan.

5. While on a low-carb diet, you're not allowed to consume fruits or vegetables. This is not true, because it's not a secret that the population for one reason or another just do not like eating fruits and vegetables. This goes back for years, and governments all over the world are now making it a point of duty by recommending the daily intakes. So, just because people have preferences doesn't mean it's down to the low-carb diet plan.

6. A low carb-diet means total elimination of carbohydrates. Even the most critical doctors,

scientists, or nutritionists will dispel this, as in any given meal, one must have at least 45% - 65% carbohydrates in their meals, depending on each individual, of course.

7. Low-carb diets will produce permanent bad breath. This to some extent is true, but not because you're on a low-carb diet plan. This is simply because, people, regardless of what weight-loss or diet program they embark on, feel they have to abstain from other meals, such as eating fruits and vegetables. Even if one's not on any form of diet, not eating fruits and vegetables will certainly attract bad breath. To combat this is simple, just eat more fruits and vegetables on a daily basis. This has nothing to do with a low-carb diet alone!

I hope with the above explanations, you can now take the plunge with ease and confidence and start embarking on a new and healthy journey and lifestyle using the low-carb diet plan.

Don't Be Confused About Low-Carb Diets

The high amounts of carbohydrates in our diet has led to increasing problems with obesity, diabetes, and other health problems. Critics, on the other hand, attribute obesity and related health problems to over-consumption of calories from any source, and lack of physical activity. Critics also express concern that the lack of grains, fruits, and vegetables in low-carbohydrate diets may lead to deficiencies of some key nutrients, including fiber, vitamin C, folic acid, and several minerals.

Any diet, whether low or high in carbohydrates, can produce significant weight-loss during the initial stages of the diet. But remember, the key to successful dieting is in being able to lose the weight permanently

Differences Between Low-Carb Diets

There are many popular diets designed to lower carbohydrate consumption. Reducing total carbohydrates in the diet means that protein and fat will represent a proportionately greater amount of the total caloric intake.

The weight loss on low-carb diets is a function of caloric restriction and diet duration, and not reduced carbohydrate intake. This finding suggests that if you want to lose weight, you should eat fewer calories and do so over a long time period.

Little evidence exists on the long-range safety of low-carb diets. Despite the medical community's concerns, no short-term adverse effects have been found on cholesterol, glucose, insulin, and blood-pressure levels among participants on the diets. But, adverse effects may not show up because of the short period of the studies. Researchers note that losing weight typically leads to an improvement in these levels anyway, and this may offset an increase caused by a high-fat diet. The long-range weight change for low-carb and other types of diets is similar.

Low-carb diets do not enable the consumption of more calories than other kinds of diets, as has been often reported. A calorie is a calorie and it doesn't matter whether they come from carbohydrates or fat. Study discrepancies are likely the result of uncontrolled circumstances; i.e. diet participants that cheat on calorie consumption, calories burned during exercise, or any number of other factors. The drop-out rate for strict (i.e. less than 40 grams of CHO/day) low-carb diets is relatively high.

What Should You Do? - There are 3 important points I would like to re-emphasize:

- The long-range success rate for low-carb and other types of diets is similar.

- Despite their popularity, little information exists on the long-term efficacy and safety of low-carbohydrate diets.

- Strict low-carb diets are usually not sustainable as a normal way of eating. Boredom usually overcomes willpower.

The diet you choose should be a blueprint for a lifetime of better eating, not just a quick weight-loss plan to reach your weight goal. If you can't see yourself eating the prescribed foods longer than a few days or a week, then chances are it's not the right diet. To this end, following a moderately low-fat diet with a healthy balance of fat, protein, carbohydrates, and other nutrients is beneficial.

If you do decide to follow a low-carb plan, remember that certain dietary fats are associated with reduction of disease. Foods high in unsaturated fats that are free of trans-fatty acids such as olive oil, fish, flaxseeds, and nuts are preferred to fats from animal origins.

Another alternative to "strict" low-carb dieting would be to give up some of the bad carbohydrate foods but not "throw out the baby with the bath water". In other words, foods high in processed sugar, snacks, and white bread would be avoided, but foods high in complex carbohydrates such as fruit, potatoes, and whole grains, retained.

1. SESAME BROILED CHICKEN

Prep time: 5 minutes

Cook time: 20 minutes

Total time: 25 minutes

Ingredients:

- 4 bone-in, skin-on chicken thighs
- ¼ teaspoon salt
- ¼ teaspoon freshly ground black pepper
- 2 tablespoons soy sauce
- 2 tablespoons sugar-free maple syrup
- 1 tablespoon sesame oil
- 1 teaspoon minced garlic
- 1 teaspoon red wine vinegar
- ½ teaspoon crushed red pepper flakes

Direction:

Season the chicken with the salt and pepper. Set aside.

In a bowl large enough to hold the chicken, combine the soy sauce, maple syrup, sesame oil, garlic, vinegar, and red pepper flakes. Reserve about one quarter of the sauce.

Add the chicken thighs to the bowl, skin-side up. Submerge in the soy sauce. Refrigerate to marinate for at least 15 minutes.

Preheat the oven to broil.

Remove the chicken from the refrigerator. Place the thighs skin-side down in the baking dish.

Place the dish in the preheated oven, about six inches from the broiler. Broil for 5 to 6 minutes with the oven door slightly ajar. Turn the chicken skin-side up. Broil for about 2 minutes more.

Turn the chicken again so it is now skin-side down. Move the baking dish to the bottom rack of the oven. Close the oven door and broil for another 6 to 8 minutes.

Turn the chicken again to skin-side up. Baste with the reserved sauce. Close the oven door and broil for 2 minutes more.

Remove the chicken from the oven. With a meat thermometer, check the internal temperature.It should reach at least 165°F.

Cool the chicken for 5 minutes before serving.

2. GREEK EGG BAKE

Prep time: 5 minutes

Cook time: 25 minutes

Total time: 30 minutes

Ingredients:

- 12 eggs
- 1 cup kale, chopped
- 1/4 cup sun-dried tomatoes
- 1/2 cup feta
- 1/2 tsp oregano
- Salt and pepper to taste
- Greek egg bake recipe

Directions:

Pre-heat the oven to 350 degrees.

Whisk together eggs.

Add in kale, tomaotes, feta, and spice.

Line a baking pan with foil (makes it easier to remove from the pan).

Spray with non-stick spray.

Bake in the oven for about 25 minutes.

Slice and serve...or portion out for the week. Will keep in the fridge for 4-5 days.

3. TURMERIC SCRAMBLED EGG

Prep Time: 5 minutes

Cook time: 6 minutes

Ingredients:

- 4 large eggs
- 2 Tbsp. milk of choice
- 2 Tsp. dried turmeric
- ½ Tsp. dried parsley
- salt& black pepper to taste
- steamed veggie of choice
- pre-cooked sausage of choice
- turmeric eggs, broccoli, and sausage

Directions:

Spray a small frying pan with nonstick cooking spray and bring to a medium heat.

In a small bowl, whisk together the eggs, milk, turmeric, parsley, salt and pepper.

Transfer the eggs to the heated pan. Cook 2-3 minutes stirring constantly to break them apart.

Flip the eggs and cook another 2-3 minutes, or until desired.

Transfer the eggs to two meal prep containers, diving them evenly. Add steamed vegetables and sausage!

4. CAULIFLOWER HASH BROWNS

Prep time: 20 minutes

Cook time: 15 minutes

Total time: 45 minutes

Ingredients:

- 1 small head grated cauliflower (about 3 cups)
- 1 large egg
- 3/4 cup shredded cheddar cheese
- 1/4 tsp cayenne pepper (optional)
- 1/4 tsp garlic powder
- 1/2 tsp pink salt
- 1/8 tsp black pepper

Directions:

Grate entire head of cauliflower.

Microwave for 3 minutes and let cool. Place in paper towels or cheese cloth and wring out all the excess water.

Place wrung out cauliflower in a bowl, add rest of ingredients and combine well.

Form into six square shaped hash browns on a greased baking tray.

Place in a 400° oven for 15-20 minutes.

Let cool for 10 minutes and hash browns will firm up. Serve warm. Enjoy!

5. BLUEBERRY PANCAKE BITES

Prep time: 15 minutes

Cook time: 25 minutes

Total time: 40 minutes

Ingredients:

- 4 large eggs
- 1/4 cup Swerve sweetener
- 1/2 tsp vanilla extract
- 1/2 cup [url]coconut flour
- 1/4 cup butter, melted
- 1 tsp baking powder
- 1/2 tsp salt
- 1/4 tsp cinnamon
- 1/3 to 1/2 cup water
- 1/2 cup Wyman's frozen wild blueberries

Directions:

Preheat oven to 325 F and grease a mini muffin tin (24 cavity) very well (double grease, first with butter and then with coconut oil spray).

In a blender combine the eggs, sweetener, and vanilla extract.Blend until smooth.

Add the coconut flour, melted butter, baking powder, salt, and cinnamon. Blend again until smooth. It will seem very liquidy but let it sit a few minutes and it will thicken up considerably. Add 1/3 cup of the water and blend again. If it's still very thick, add a little additional water. You shouldn't be able to pour it, but you should be able to scoop it out of the blender easily.

Divide among the prepared muffin cups. Add a few blueberries to each. Press them gently into the batter.

Bake 20 to 25 minutes, until set. Let cool a few minutes in the pan and then serve with your favourite low carb pancake syrup.

6. KETO BAGELS

Prep time: 15 minutes

Cook time: 14 minutes

Ingredients:

- 2 cups almond flour
- 1 tbsp baking powder
- 1 tsp garlic powder
- 1 tsp onion powder
- 1 tsp dried Italian seasoning
- 3 large eggs, divided
- 3 cups shredded low moisture mozzarella cheese
- 5 tbsp cream cheese
- 3 tbsp Everything Bagel Seasoning

Directions:

Preheat oven to 425°.Line a rimmed baking sheet with parchment paper or a Silpat.

In a medium mixing bowl, combine the almond flour, baking powder, garlic powder, onion powder, and dried Italian seasoning. Mix until well combined, put the mixture through a flour sifter to ensure that all the baking powder gets mixed in with the rest of the ingredients.

Crack one of the eggs into a small bowl and fork whisk. This will be the egg wash for the top of the bagels. The other two eggs will go in the dough.

In a large microwave safe mixing bowl, combine the mozzarella cheese and cream cheese. Microwave for 1 minute and 30 seconds. Remove from microwave and stir to combine. Return to microwave for 1 additional minute. Mix until well combined.

To the mixing bowl, add the remaining 2 eggs and the almond flour mixture. Mix until all ingredients are well incorporated. If the dough gets too stringy and unworkable, simply put it back in the microwave for 30 seconds to soften and continue mixing.

Divide the dough into 6 equal portions.Roll each portion into a ball.

Gently press your finger into the center of each dough ball to form a ring. Stretch the ring to make a small hole in the center and form it into a bagel shape.

Brush the top of each bagel with the egg wash.

Top each bagel with Everything Bagel Seasoning.

Bake on the middle rack for 12-14 minutes or until golden brown.

7. LOW-CARB BREAKFAST PIZZA

Prep time: 10 minutes

Cook time: 30 minutes

Total time: 40 minutes

Ingredients:

- 12 eggs
- 1/2 cup heavy cream
- 1/2 tsp salt
- 1/4 tsp pepper
- 8 oz sausage
- 2 cups peppers, sliced
- 1 cup cheese, shredded

Directions:

Preheat oven to 350°.

Add peppers to microwave for 3 minutes.

Brown sausage in cast iron skillet.

Take out and set aside.

Mix eggs, cream, salt and pepper together and add to skillet.

Cook for 5 minutes until the sides start to set up.

Add to oven and bake for 15 minutes.

Take out and add sausage, peppers and cheese.

Set under broiler for 3 minutes.

8. KETO BACON SAUSAGE MEATBALLS

Prep time: 10 minutes

Cook time: 30 minutes

Ingredients:

- 1 pound spicy italian sausage whole 30, if needed
- 9 sliced sugar-free bacon
- 2 tbsp garlic, minced
- 2 tbsp white onion diced
- 1 tbsp dried oregano

Directions:

Preheat oven to 375 F. Prepare a standard muffin pan by greasing 9 cavities lightly with coconut oil.

In a large mixing bowl, combine the Italian sausage, garlic, onion and oregano.

Roll the mixture into 9 equal balls with your hands and place on a plate.

Wrap each ball with a slice of bacon then place each one in a muffin cavity.

Bake at 375 F for 30 minutes then cook under a high broiler for 5 minutes to get the bacon crispy.

Remove from the oven and prepare.

9. CREAM CHEESE & SALAMI KETO PINWHEELS

Ingredients:

- 1 8oz block cream cheese
- 8-10 thin slices of pepperoni and genoa salami ,may need more depending on size
- 4 tbsp finely diced pickles

Directions:

Bring cream cheese to room temperature and whip until fluffy.

Spread cream cheese in a 1/4 inch thick rectangle in the center of a large piece of plastic wrap.

Spread pickles over cream cheese.

Place salami over cream cheese in overlapping layers so all cream cheese layer is covered.

Place a second piece of plastic wrap over salami layer and gently press down.

Flip entire rectangle over so bottom cream cheese layer is now facing the top.

Carefully peel back plastic wrap off top cream cheese layer.

Begin rolling into log shape slowly removing bottom layer of plastic wrap as you go.

Place pinwheel in tight plastic wrap and refrigerate at least 4 hours, overnight preferred.

Slice into preferred thickness.

10. CHEESEBURGER LETTUCE WRAPS

Prep time: 15 minutes

Cook time: 8 minutes

Total time: 23 minutes

Ingredients:

- 2 pounds lean ground beef
- 1/2 tsp seasoned salt
- 1 tsp black pepper
- 1 tsp dried oregano
- 6 slices American cheese
- 2 large heads iceburg or romaine lettuce, rinsed then dried
- 2 tomatoes, sliced thin
- small red onion, sliced thin
- Spread:1/4 cup light mayo
- 3 tbsp ketchup
- 1 tbsp dill pickle relish
- dash of salt and pepper

Directions:

Heat a grill or skillet on medium heat.

In a large bowl, mix together ground beef, seasoned salt, pepper and oregano.

Divide mixture into 6 sections then roll each into a ball. Press each ball down flat to form a patty.

Place patties on grill/pan and cook for approximately 4 minutes on each side or until cooked to your liking. (If using a skillet, only cook 3 at a time to avoid over-crowding.)

Place a slice of cheese on each cooked burger. Place each burger on a large piece of lettuce. Top with spread , one slice tomato, red onion and whatever else you like. Wrap the lettuce up over the top and serve.

Spread: In a small bowl mix together all the spread ingredients. Refrigerate until ready to use.

11. SESAME SALMON WITH BABY BOK CHOY AND MUSHROOMS

Ingredients:

Main Dish

- 4 each 4-6 oz.salmon fillet
- 2 each portobello mushroom caps (or 8 oz. baby bella mushrooms)
- 4 each baby bok choy
- 1 tbsp toasted sesame seeds
- 1 each green onion

Marinade

- 1 tbsp olive oil
- 1 tsp sesame oil
- 1 tbsp coconut aminos
- 1/2 inch ginger grated (approx. 1 tsp.)
- 1/2 lemon juice
- 1/2 tsp salt
- 1/2 tsp black pepper

Directions:

Whisk together all of your marinade ingredients.

Drizzle half of the marinade on the salmon and turn to coat. Cover and refrigerate the salmon while it marinates for one hour.

Preheat oven to 400.

Prepare vegetables: Trim the rough ends from the bok choy and cut into halves. Slice the mushrooms into ½ inch pieces.

Drizzle the remaining marinade over the vegetables and lay on a lined baking sheet.

Place salmon, skin side down, on a lined baking sheet as well. Bake until salmon is cooked through, about 20 minutes.

Top with sliced green onions and sesame seeds.

12. BACON, CHICKEN & TOMATO STUFFED AVOCADO

Prep time: 10 minutes

Cook time: 20 minutes

Total time: 30 minutes

Ingredients:

- 2 chicken breasts, grilled
- 3 pieces bacon, cooked and chopped
- 2 avocado
- 1/3 cup grape tomatoes, chopped
- 1/3 cup mayo, paleo

Directions:

Sprinkle chicken with favorite seasoning, grill, and cut into cubes.

Grill bacon strips, and set aside.

Place cubed chicken in a medium bowl. Add tomatoes, onions and bacon.

Add Paleo Mayo and gently mix everything together.

Just before serving, slice avocados in half and discard pit.

Pile the chicken mix on top of each avocado half.

13. KETO CHICKEN ENCHILADA BOWL

Ingredients:

- 2-3 chicken breasts (about one pound of chicken)
- 3/4 cups red enchilada sauce
- 1/4 cup water
- 1/4 cup onion
- 1 4 oz can green chiles
- 1 12oz steam bag cauliflower rice
- Preferred toppings- use avocado, jalapeno, cheese, and roma tomatoes, seasoning to taste.

Directions:

In skillet over medium heat cook chicken breasts until lightly brown.

Add enchilada sauce, chiles, onions, water and reduce heat to simmer, covered.

Cover and cook until chicken is cooked through and shred chicken.

Add chicken back into sauce and continue simmering for additional 10 minutes uncovered or until most of liquid has been soaked up.

Prepare cauliflower rice per bag instructions and dice preferred toppings.

Top rice with chicken, cheese, avocado or preferred toppings.

14. AVOCADO TUNA SALAD RECIPE

Prep time: 10 minutes

Ingredients

- 15 oz tuna in oil, drained and flaked (3 small cans)
- 1 English cucumber, sliced
- 2 large or 3 medium avocados peeled, pitted & sliced
- 1 small/medium red onion thinly sliced
- 1/4 cup cilantro (1/2 of a small bunch)
- 2 tbsp lemon juice freshly squeezed
- 2 tbsp extra virgin olive oil
- 1 tsp sea salt or to taste
- 1/8 tsp black pepper

Directions

In a large salad bowl, combine: sliced cucumber, sliced avocado, thinly sliced red onion, drained tuna, and 1/4 cup cilantro

Drizzle salad ingredients with 2 tbsp lemon juice, 2 tbsp olive oil, 1 tsp salt and 1/8 tsp black pepper (or season to taste). Toss to combine and serve.

15. SHEET PAN CHICKEN FAJITAS

Prep time: 15 minutes

Cook time: 20 minutes

Total time: 35 minutes

Ingredients:

- 1.5 lbs chicken breasts, boneless, skinless
- olive oil
- 1 tbsp taco seasoning
- 3 bell peppers, sliced
- 1 onion, sliced thinly
- fresh limes

Directions:

Preheat oven to 400ºF and grease large rimmed baking sheet.

Slice chicken into strips and season to coat with taco seasoning. Lightly drizzle seasoned chicken with olive oil.

Chop all veggies into strips. Drizzle with olive oil and more taco seasoning if desired.

Place chicken and veggies on sheet pan and bake at 400 F until chicken strips are cooked through and veggies are tender, about 20-25 minutes

Remove from oven and squeeze fresh lime over. Serve as desired in tortillas or over cauliflower rice.

16. SPICY MUSTARD THYME CHICKEN & COCONUT ROASTED BRUSSELS SPROUTS

Prep time: 10 minutes

Cook time: 25 minutes

Ingredients:

- 1 pound Brussels sprouts sliced in half
- 2 medium boneless skinless chicken breast
- 1/4 cup ground spicy mustard
- 1 tbsp lemon juice
- 1 tsp thyme
- Salt & pepper to taste
- 1 tbsp coconut oil, melted

Directions:

In a small ramekin, whisk together the spicy mustard with lemon juice, salt, pepper, and thyme.

Place the two chicken breasts in a bowl and pour the mustard over them. Using a spoon, coat the chicken breasts with the mustard. Place in the refrigerator to marinate 10 minutes then remove and bring to room temperature 15 minutes prior to cooking.

Preheat oven to 350 F. Prepare a baking sheet with parchment paper.

Next, place Brussels sprouts in a medium bowl and toss with melted coconut oil, salt and pepper.

Transfer Brussels sprouts to the prepared baking sheets, spreading into an even layer.

Place marinated chicken breasts in a glass baking pan.

Place the chicken breasts in the oven baking at 350 F 10 minutes. After 10 minutes, place the Brussels sprouts in the oven.Cook both 15 minutes.

Remove from the oven and divide the meal into two servings, placing in individual meal prep containers.

17. FATHEAD PIZZA CRUST RECIPE (LOW-CARB KETO PIZZA)

Prep time: 10 minutes

Cook time: 10 minutes

Total time: 20 minutes

This low carb keto Fathead pizza crust recipe with coconut flour is so easy, with only 4 ingredients, it's the ultimate keto pizza - easy to make, chewy, and ready in 20 minutes.

Ingredients:

- 1 1/2 cup mozzarella cheese, shredded
- 2 tbsp cream cheese cut into cubes
- 2 large eggs, beaten
- 1/3 cups coconut flour

Directions:

Preheat the oven to 425° F . Line a baking sheet or pizza pan with parchment paper.

Combine the shredded mozzarella and cubed cream cheese in a large bowl. Microwave for 90 seconds, stirring halfway through. Stir again at the end until well incorporated (**see notes for an alternative to the microwave).

Stir in the beaten eggs and coconut flour. Knead with your hands until a dough forms. If the dough becomes hard before fully mixed, you can microwave for 10-15 seconds to soften it.

Spread the dough onto the lined baking pan to 1/4" or 1/3" thickness, using your hands or a rolling pin over a piece of parchment (the rolling pin works better if you have one). Use a toothpick or fork to poke lots of holes throughout the crust to prevent bubbling.

Bake for 6 minutes. Poke more holes in any places where you see bubbles forming. Bake for 3-7 more minutes, until golden brown.

Recipe notes:

To make a keto pizza, top with sauce and toppings after cooking the crust and return to the oven for about 10 minutes, until heated through.

**If you don't want to use the microwave, use a double boiler to melt the cheese and cream cheese together instead. Boil water in a saucepan, then place the cheeses in a metal bowl resting over the edges of the saucepan. The idea is to melt the cheese without burning it, stirring frequently.

Nutrition info does not include toppings.

18. KETO LASAGNA WITH ZUCCHINI NOODLES

Prep time: 15 minutes

Cook time: 30 minutes

Total time: 45 minutes

Ingredients:

- 16 oz ground beef
- 1 cup Rao's marinara sauce
- 1 zucchini, large
- 10 oz ricotta cheese
- 4 oz mozzarella cheese, shredded

Directions:

Preheat oven to 350° F. Peel zucchini into strips and leave out the seedy core. Salt and let sit for 15 minutes and blot with paper towels.

Brown ground beef in pan and add marinara. Season well with salt and pepper.

Layer into a small casserole dish: meat, zucchini, ricotta, meat, zucchini, ricotta, mozzarella.

Cover with foil and bake for 30 minutes. Broil uncovered for 2-3 minutes to brown the top.

19. ONE-PAN LEMON CHICKEN WITH ASPARAGUS

Prep time: 5 minutes

Cook time: 25 minutes

Total time: 30 minutes

The method here is simple enough: coat your chicken in light flour batter. You can use a regular gluten free flour or tapioca/arrowroot if you're looking for a grain free.

After you brown the chicken on both sides, you quickly braise the asparagus in the pan along with a little garlic, stock, lemon juice and mustard. Once the sauce reduces down you simply add the chicken back to the pan, sprinkle with some parsley for added freshness and you're done. All done in less than 30 minutes and in one pan.

Serve the lemon chicken & asparagus over a bed of rice/cauliflower rice to soak up all the saucy goodness. Bright and punchy lemon garlic flavours with a tangy, mustard bite .

Ingredients:

- 4 chicken breasts, boneless, skinless
- 1/4 cup tapioca flour for paleo or plain gluten-free flour
- 2 tbsp olive oil
- 3/4 tsp sea salt plus more for seasoning
- 1/2 tsp ground black pepper plus more for seasoning
- 1 pound asparagus stalks ends trimmed and then cut in half
- 2 cloves garlic crushed
- 3 tbsp fresh lemon juice
- 1/2 zest of lemon
- 1 tbsp dijon mustard
- 1 cup chicken stock aim for a lower sodium stock
- 1 tbsp fresh parsley roughly chopped, plus more for garnishing

Directions:

Place the chicken breasts between two pieces of plastic cling wrap and pound them down to make them even in thickness. This will help the chicken cook evenly and make for more tender chicken. If your breasts are extra thick you can also just cut/slice them in half.

Place the flour, salt & pepper in a shallow dish and gently toss the chicken breasts to coat in flour.

In a large skillet add one tablespoon of olive oil and bring to a medium-high heat. When the oil is hot add the chicken to the skillet and cook each side for about 5 minutes or until golden and cooked through. Once cooked remove the chicken and place on a paper towel lined plate. Set aside while you cook the asparagus.

Add the remaining 1 tablespoon olive oil in the skillet. Add the asparagus stalks and sauté for a minute. Add the garlic and sauté another minute longer until fragrant.

In a small bowl or cup whisk together the lemon juice and mustard until fully mixed.Pour into the skillet with the asparagus along with the chicken stock and the zest. Bring the liquid to a boil and then reduce down to a simmer. Cover and let cook another 3-4 minutes or until the asparagus is tender.

Stir in the parsley and then add the chicken back to the pan and rotate the breasts to coat in the liquids. Taste the sauce and season with more salt & pepper as needed.

20 . CHEESY BACON-STUFFED MINI PEPPERS

Prep time: 15 minutes

Cook time: 12 minutes

Total time: 27 minutes

These Cheesy Bacon-Stuffed Mini Peppers are the perfect crowd pleasing appetizer. They're stuffed with two kinds of cheese, bacon, and more, then baked till melty and delicious!

Ingredients:

6 mini sweet peppers sliced in half, seeds and membranes removed

4 oz cream cheese

2 tbsp green onions, sliced

4 slices bacon, cooked and crumbled

1/2 tsp garlic powder

1/2 cup shredded cheddar cheese, plus extra for topping

1 tsp Worcestershire sauce

chopped cilantro for topping (optional)

Directions:

Preheat oven to 400°. Spray a cookie sheet with nonstick cooking spray and set aside.

In a small bowl, beat together the cream cheese, green onions, bacon, garlic powder, cheddar, and worcestershire sauce with an electric mixer until smooth.

Fill the sliced peppers with the filling, about a heaping tablespoon each. Place on prepared cookie sheet, then sprinkle each pepper with a little extra cheese. Bake in the preheated oven for 10-12 minutes until cheese is melted and bubbly and peppers have softened.

Allow to cool slightly before eating. Sprinkle with a little chopped cilantro if desired.

21. STEAK BITES

Prep time: 10 minuts

Cook time: 3 minuts

Marinate time: 3-24 hours

Ingredients:

- 1/2 cup soy sauce
- 1/3 cup olive oil
- 1/4 cup Worcestershire sauce
- 1 tsp minced garlic
- 2 tbsp dried basil
- 1 tbsp dried parsley
- 1 tsp black pepper
- 1-1/2 lbs flat iron or top sirloin steak, cut in 1-inch pieces

Directions:

Place all ingredients, except steak, in a large ziplock baggie. Stir with a spoon to combine.

Drop steak pieces in and seal shut. Shake gently to coat steak entirely in marinade.Place bag in refrigerator to marinate for at least 3 hours or up to 24.

Heat a large skillet over medium-high heat. Heat skillet until it's very hot. Remove steak pieces from marinade using a slotted spoon and place in hot skillet. Discard marinade. Cook steak according to your desired temperature.We like medium-well so I cooked ours for about 3 minutes.

22. KETO AVOCADO BROWNIES

Prep time: 10 minutes

Cook time: 35 minutes

Total time: 45 minutes

Ingredients:

- 250 g avocado about 2
- 1/2 tsp vanilla
- 4 tbsp cocoa powder
- 1 tsp stevia powder
- 3 tbsp refined coconut oil
- 2 eggs
- 100 g Lily's Dark Chocolate, melted
- 90 g blanched almond flour
- 1/4 tsp baking soda
- 1 tsp baking powder
- 1/4 tsp salt
- 1/4 cup erythritol

Directions:

Preheat the oven to 350F.

Peel the avocados and place in a food processor. Process until smooth.

Add each ingredient one at a time and process for a few seconds until all of the ingredients (except the dry ones) have been added to the food processor.

In a separate bowl, combine the dry ingredients together and whisk together. Add to the food processor and mix until combined.

Place a piece of parchment paper over a 30x20cm baking dish and pour the batter into it. Spoon evenly and place in the preheated oven. Bake for 35 minutes.

Take out of the oven, let cool and slice into 12 pieces.

23. COCONUT OIL FAT BOMBS

Prep time: 15 minutes

Cook time: 5 minutes

Total time: 20 minutes

These 5-ingredient coconut oil bombs melt in your mouth and pack a dose of energy!

Ingredients:

- 2 cups shredded unsweetened coconut
- 1/3 cup coconut oil, melted
- 2 tbsp raw honey
- 4 oz raw dark chocolate chips
- 1/2 tsp vanilla bean powder, optional

Directions:

In a blender, add shredded coconut, coconut oil, raw honey and vanilla bean powder. Blend until mixture is fine and crumbled.

Line a small baking sheet or plate with wax paper. Using a tablespoon-size measuring spoon, scoop mixture and form into small mounds, using your hands. Set onto wax paper.Place in freezer 10 minutes to set. Using a double boiler, melt chocolate until smooth. Use a butterknife to drizzle coconut bombs with chocolate. Place back into refrigerator to set 10 minutes. Store in refrigerator.

24. KETO BREAD

Total time: 40 minutes

Ingredients:

- 1½ cups almond flour
- 6 egg whites
- ¼ tsp cream of tartar
- 3–4 tbsp butter, melted
- ¾ tsp baking soda
- 3 tsp apple cider vinegar
- 2 tbsp coconut flour

Directions:

Preheat oven to 375 F.

The first thing you'll need to do is separate six eggs. You'll only use the egg whites for this keto bread recipe, so feel free to set the yolks off to the side to save for another recipe. Add the cream of tartar to the egg whites and, using a hand mixer, whip the eggs until soft peaks are formed.

Add the almond flour, butter, baking soda, apple cider vinegar and coconut flour to a food processor, blending until well-incorporated.

Place the mix into a bowl and gently fold in the egg white mixture.

Grease an 8x4 loaf pan and pour in the bread mixture.

Bake for 30 minutes.

Your loaf should come out just browned on top!

Allow the bread to cool slightly before cutting into it. Then, serve and enjoy!

25. AVOCADO DEVILED EGGS RECIPE — THE IDEAL KETO SNACK

Total time: 25 minutes

Ingredients:

- 4–6 eggs
- 1 avocado
- ¼ tsp sea salt
- ¼ tsp pepper
- ¼ tsp garlic
- ¼ tsp chili powder
- ¼ tsp cumin
- ¼ tsp smoked paprika, optional*
- 2 tbsp cilantro

Directions:

In a medium pot add eggs and cover with water until fully submerged.

Bring to a boil, then remove from heat and cover for 12–13 minutes.

Fill a large bowl with ice water and, using a slotted spoon, gently place eggs in the bowl, allowing eggs to chill for 5 minutes.

Remove outer casing from eggs and slice in half lengthwise, removing the yolk.

Add the yolk, along with the avocado and spices to a bowl, mixing together until well combined.

Add the mixture to the egg halves.

Drizzle with lime juice and top with cilantro.

Benefit-rich eggs are a serious powerhouse food. They're a relatively inexpensive source of meat-free protein that can help prevent disease, improve eye health and help you drop pounds. And while they're most often enjoyed as a breakfast food or a baking ingredient, they make a pretty tasty and popular appetizer in the form of deviled eggs.

26. CHOCOLATE FAT BOMBS RECIPE

Prep time: 10 minuts

Total time: 25 minuts

Ingredients:

- 125g/4.4 oz cream cheese
- 125g/4.4 oz unsalted butter
- 2 tbsp cacao powder
- 1 tbsp sweetener of choice (or more to taste)

Directions:

Place the cream cheese and butter into a large bowl and allow to soften gently at room temperature.

When softened beat briefly with an electric whisk then add the cacao powder and your sweetener of choice.

Beat until smooth.

Get out mini baking cups and place 1-2 teaspoons of the mixture into each cup.

Place into the fridge to firm and enjoy!

27. CAULIFLOWER-CRUSTED GRILLED CHEESE SANDWICHES

Ingredients:

- 1 medium head of cauliflower (raw), cut into small florets and stems removed
- 1 large egg
- 1/2 cup shredded Parmesan cheese
- 1 tsp Italian herb seasoning
- 2 thick slices of white cheddar cheese (you can also use shredded cheddar cheese)

Directions:

Preheat oven to 450F. Place cauliflower into food processor and pulse until crumbs about half the size of a grain of rice.

Place cauliflower into large microwave safe bowl and microwave for 2 minutes. Your cauliflower should be soft and tender (and hot!). (If you don't want to use the microwave to dry out the cauliflower and prefer to steam and wring with a cloth to dry.)

Stir cauliflower to mix up the bottom and top cauliflower. Place back into the microwave and cook for another 3 minutes. Remove and stir again so that all the cauliflower cooks evenly. Place back into microwave and cook for 5 minutes. At this point, you should see the cauliflower is starting to become more dry. Microwave for another 5 minutes. Cauliflower should still be slightly moist to the touch, but should look dry and clumped up, If you've made cauliflower pizza or breadsticks with the cloth wringing dry method,

Allow cauliflower to cool for a few minutes. Then add in egg and cheese. Stir to combine until smooth paste forms. Stir in seasoning. Divide dough into 4 equal parts. Place onto large baking sheet lined with parchment paper.Using your knuckles and fingers, shape into square bread slices about 1/3 inch thick.Bake cauliflower bread for about 15-18 minutes or until golden brown. Remove from oven and let cool a few minutes.

Using a good spatula, carefully slide cauliflower bread off of parchment paper. Now you are ready to assemble your sandwiches. You can do this a few different ways. You can either cook on the stove top as you would normally cook a grilled cheese. You can also place sandwiches into toaster oven and broil for several minutes (5-10) until cheese is completely melted and bread is toasty. If you don't own a toaster oven, you can also do this in the oven.

28. CHICKEN PAD THAI

Prep time: 20 minutes

Cook time: 10 minutes

Total time: 30 minutes

This chicken pad thai recipe is extremely healthy and nutritious meal, it can be prepared ahead of time.

Ingredients:

- ⅛ tsp ground ginger
- ⅛ tsp garlic powder
- ⅛ tsp sea salt
- ⅛ tsp freshly ground black pepper
- 2 pounds free-range chicken tenders
- 2 tbsp peanut oil
- 3 large free-range eggs, lightly beaten
- ⅓ cup organic chicken broth
- 3 tbsp peanut butter
- 2 tbsp tamari
- 1 tbsp rice vinegar
- ½ cup chopped scallion

- 2 garlic cloves, minced
- 1 tsp red pepper flakes
- 4 zucchini, spiralized
- ½ cup bean sprouts
- ½ cup crushed peanuts, for garnish
- 1 lime, cut into wedges, for garnish

Directions:

In a medium bowl, mix the ginger, garlic powder, salt, and black pepper. Add the chicken tenders and toss until coated.

In a medium skillet, heat the peanut oil over medium-high heat. When the oil is hot, add the chicken tenders and cook, turning once, until cooked through, about 3 minutes. Remove the chicken from the skillet and cut into ¼-inch-thick slices.Set aside.

Add the eggs to the skillet and scramble them for about 1 minute. Remove the scrambled eggs from the skillet and set aside.

Reduce the heat under the skillet to medium-low and add the chicken broth, peanut butter, tamari, vinegar, scallion, garlic, and red pepper flakes. Stir well and cook for 3 minutes.

Add the chicken slices, zucchini noodles, scrambled eggs, and sprouts to the skillet. Toss to coat with the sauce, and cook for about 1 minute.

Serve the pad thai garnished with the peanuts and lime wedges.

29. CINNAMON BUTTER FAT BOMBS

Ingredients:

- 1 lb salted butter, preferably grass-fed

- 1/4 cup honey (OR, substitute all or part of the honey with your favorite low-calorie sweetener to taste; personally I like 1 tablespoon honey and 20 drops SweetLeaf clear liquid stevia)

- 1 tbsp cinnamon

- 1 1/2 tsp vanilla extract

- Salt to taste, if using unsalted butter

Directions:

Allow butter to soften on your counter until it is slightly squishy.

Add butter, cinnamon, honey/stevia, and vanilla extract to your food processor. Process for a couple of minutes to mix ingredients and achieve slightly whipped taste. Stop food processor as necessary to scrape down the bowl and reincorporate ingredients.

Spoon butter mixture into silicone molds, Alternatively, you can line a cutting board or other flat surface with parchment paper and then spoon dollops of butter mixture onto the parchment paper.

Freeze for an hour or two, then remove from parchment paper or molds and store in a container in your freeze.

30. COCONUT OIL MAYONNAISE

Total time: 10 minutes

Ingredients:

- 2 egg yolks at room temperature
- 1 tsp mustard
- 2 tsp fresh lemon juice
- ½ cup olive oil
- ¾ cup of coconut oil, melted
- pinch of sea salt and black pepper

Directions:

In a blender, add egg yolks, mustard, 1 teaspoon fresh lemon juice and blend on very low setting.

Slowly drizzle in the oil while blender is still on low speed.

Once oil is well incorporated, add the remaining lemon juice.

Add salt and pepper, to taste.

Place mayo in a jar and store in the refrigerator.

31. CREAMY CAULIFLOWER MASH AND KETO GRAVY

Total time: 1 hour

Ingredients:

- 5 cups cauliflower chopped
- 4 tbsp heavy whipping cream
- 3 tbsp Butter
- 5 cloves garlic minced
- 2 tsp dried rosemary
- 3 tbsp parmesan
- 1/2 tsp pepper
- Pink salt (to taste)

Directions:

Chop up 5 cups of raw cauliflower.

Bring pot of water to a boil (enough to cover all the cauliflower), add the cauliflower and boil for 15 minutes or until tender.

Drain cauliflower and place in processor.

Cook butter, garlic and rosemary in a saucepan over medium heat until fragrant.

Add melted butter, garlic and rosemary to processor and pulse several times until well combined.

Add cream, parmesan, salt and pepper to processor and process until smooth and creamy.

Taste for salt level. Serve warm.

32. CRUSTLESS SPINACH QUICHE RECIPE

Total time: 40 minutes

Ingredients:

- 1 tbsp coconut oil
- 1 onion, chopped
- 1 package frozen chopped spinach, thawed and drained
- 8 eggs, beaten
- 3 cups shredded raw cheese
- ¼ tsp sea salt
- ⅛ tsp black pepper

Directions:

Preheat oven to 350° F and grease a 9 inch pie pan with coconut oil.

Heat coconut oil, and onions over medium heat in sauce pan until onions are soft. Stir in spinach and cook until excess moisture has evaporated.

In a bowl, combine eggs, cheese, salt and pepper.
Add spinach mixture and blend.

Scoop into pan and bake for 30 minutes.

33. SIMPLE PALEO CHICKEN CURRY RECIPE

Prep time: 30 minutes

Cook time: 30 minutes

Ingredients:

- 2 tbsp coconut oil (or oil of your choice)
- 8 chicken thighs ,boneless skinless, cut into 1" pieces
- 1 large onion, cut into large chunks
- 3 small zucchini, cut half lengthwise and thickly sliced
- 1 tsp garlic, minced
- 1 tbsp curry powder
- 1/2 tsp paprika
- 2 tsp salt
- 2 cans coconut milk (about 15 oz each)
- 1 cup tomatoes
- cilantro (to garnish)

Directions:

Heat the olive oil in a stock pot to high heat. Add the chicken and cook until chicken pieces are browned on both sides. Remove the chicken from the pan and set aside, keeping the remaining oil in the stock pot.

Add the onion and zucchini and saute until lightly browned. Add the garlic, curry powder, paprika, and salt and saute for 30 seconds.

Add the chicken back into the pot, along with the coconut milk. Bring to a boil.

Reduce heat to a simmer, cover the pot with a lid, and let simmer for 30 minutes, or until chicken is tender. Add the tomatoes to the pot in the last 5 minutes of cooking.

Serve in a bowl with the coconut broth, like a soup.Top with cilantro.

34. CAULIFLOWER MAC AND CHEESE

Total time: 30-40 minutes

Ingredients:

- 1 large cauliflower head, cut into small florets
- ½-¾ cup kefir
- ½ cup goat's milk cottage cheese, pureed
- 1½ tsp Dijon mustard
- 1½ cups grated sheep's or goat's milk cheddar cheese, plus additional for topping
- ½ tsp black pepper
- 1 tsp sea salt
- ⅛ tsp garlic powder

Directions:

Preheat oven to 375° F. Grease 8" x 8" pan with ghee.

Bring a pot of salted water to a boil. Add cauliflower and cook until slightly tender, about 5 minutes. Drain and pat dry with paper towels. Spread in prepared pan.

In a saucepan over medium-high heat, mix together kefir, cottage cheese, and mustard until smooth.

In a saucepan over medium high heat, mix together the cottage cheese, kefir and mustard until smooth

Stir in cheese, sea salt, black pepper, and garlic powder until cheese just starts to melt. Pour over cauliflower and stir. Top with additional cheese if desired and bake for 10–15 minutes.

35. JALAPENO CHEDDAR BURGERS (TURKEY OR BEEF)

Prep time: 15 miunutes

Cook time: 15 minutes

Total time: 30 minutes

Ingredients:

- 28 oz lean turkey or beef (not extra lean)
- 2 tbsp finely minced onion
- salt & pepper to taste
- 4 tbsp cream cheese
- 2 oz shredded cheddar cheese
- 1/4 tsp garlic powder
- 1 fresh jalapeno pepper, diced (seeds removed if you prefer less spice)
- 1 tbsp olive oil
- Rolls & Toppings as desired

Directions:

Preheat grill to medium or oven to broil on high.

In a small bowl combine cream cheese, cheddar cheese, garlic powder and diced jalapeno.

Combine meat, salt & pepper and minced onion. Divide meat into 4 even pieces (7oz each). Take 1/4 of the cream cheese mixture and flatten it into a pancake shape. Wrap beef or turkey around the cheese ensuring the cheese mixture is completely covered. Brush each burger with a little bit of olive oil.

To Grill:

Grill burgers over medium heat for 6-7 minutes on each side or until completely cooked. (Turkey should reach an internal temperature of 165 degrees and beef should reach 160° F.)

To Broil:

Place burgers on a foil covered pan approximately 6" from the broiler. Broil 5-6 minutes on each side or until completely cooked. (Turkey should reach an

internal temperature of 165° and beef should reach
160° F.)

36. ONION SOUP

Total time: 45–60 minutes

Ingredients:

- 4 large onions, peeled and thinly sliced
- 2 cups chicken bone broth
- 2 cups beef bone broth
- 4 tbsp ghee
- 5 garlic cloves, chopped
- Goat cheese, for topping (optional)
- Sea salt and black pepper to taste

Directions:

In a stock pot over medium heat, melt ghee and thinly sliced onions.

Cook onions until lightly caramelized.

Add bone broth and garlic.

Season with salt and pepper to taste.

Bring mixture to a boil and then reduce the heat and allow to simmer for 30–50 minutes (the longer, the more flavor).

Soup, glorious soup. It's such an easy way to start a multi-course meal or, paired with a side salad and sprouted bread, a simple lunch or dinner. And there's no better — or easier — soup than this onion soup recipe. You've likely had French onion when out, or maybe even from a can, but no more. With this easy onion soup recipe, you can enjoy homemade, healthy onion soup whenever the mood strikes.

37. BABA GANOUSH

Prep time: 20 minutes

Total time: 30 minutes

Ingredients:

- 1 eggplant, sliced
- 1 cup tahini
- 3–4 garlic cloves, smashed
- 1–2 tbsp avocado oil
- 1 cup parsley, chopped
- Sea salt and pepper to taste

Directions:

On a baking sheet lined with parchment paper, lay out the eggplant slices.

Salt the eggplant and allow eggplant to sit for 15–20 minutes to remove moisture.

Use a paper towel to dab eggplant, removing excess water.

Broil eggplant on top oven rack for 5–8 minutes.

Remove skin (optional).

Place eggplant in a food processor and pulse until broken down.

Place all other ingredients in the food processor and blend on high until well combined.

Serve with chopped vegetables.

38. PIZZA GRILLED CHICKEN

Prep time: 15 minutes

Cook time: 15 minutes

Total time: 25 minutes

Ingredients:

- 1 boneless skinless chicken breast
- 1/2 tbsp olive oil
- 1 clove garlic, minced
- 1/2 cup half & half or heavy whipping cream
- 1/4 tsp xanthan gum thickener
- 1 cup fresh spinach, roughly chopped
- 1/2 cup part-skim shredded mozzarella
- Sea salt & pepper to taste

Fathead Dough:

- 2oz cream cheese
- 3/4 cup shredded mozzarella
- 1 egg, beaten
- 1/4 tsp garlic powder

- 1/3 cup almond flour

Directions:

To make the pizza crust,

Melt mozzarella and cream cheese in the microwave for 30 seconds at a time. Mixing often.

In a separate bowl mix beaten egg with almond flour and remaining dough ingredients.

Combine cheese mixture with flour and mix. Mix. Keep mixing! Once a sticky dough consistency has been reached, refrigerate while preparing sauce and chicken.

Saute the chicken in a skillet over medium heat until done.Remove, set aside.

Add garlic plus the xantham gum with half & half to the skillet and bring to a boil. Reduce to simmer when sauce starts to thicken.

Fold in spinach, cook just until wilted.

Using hands, work dough out into a circle on a pizza pan. Bake on 350 for 10 minutes. Crust must be pre-baked to hold up to the sauce and toppings.

Spread sauce/spinach mixture onto your cooked pizza crust. Top with chicken and shredded cheese

Bake 5 minutes or until cheese is melted.

NOTE* if your oven and pizza crust weren't already hot from making the dough, bake for 10 minutes instead.

39. BURGER COOK MUSHROOOM

Ingredients:

- 1 pound grass fed beef

- 24 baby portabella mushrooms

- 4 slices sharp cheddar, sliced into quarters

- 4 tbsp chopped yellow onion

- 2 dill pickles, sliced

- 2 tbsp extra virgin olive oil

- 12 basil leaves

- yellow mustard, mayo, sriracha or low carb ketchup (optional)

- salt and pepper to taste

Directions:

Remove stems from portabella mushroom caps and wipe with a damp paper towel to remove any dirt or debris. In a small saucepan, heat 1 tablespoon olive oil over medium heat. Add mushroom caps and cook for 2 minutes on each side, allowing mushrooms to cook through but retain firmness.

Remove mushrooms from pan and place on paper towels to allow liquid to drain off.

Divide the ground beef into 12 portions, rolling each into a small disc shape. Add salt and pepper to taste. In a large grill pan, heat remaining tbsp olive oil over medium heat. Once the pan is hot, add the meat and allow to cook for 3 minutes on one side. Flip and allow to cook for 3 minutes on the other side. Cook to desired level of doneness.

Stack a mushroom, burger, cheese, onion, pickles and your choice of condiments. Top with second mushroom cap and add a basil leaf for garnish. Use a toothpick to hold.

40. EASY CHOCOLATE MOUSSE

Ingredients:

- 8 oz cream cheese block, softened

- ¼ cup unsweetened cocoa powder

- ½ large avocado, pitted

- ⅛ tsp vanilla extract

- 2-3 tbsp of desired sweetener, I recommend Swerve.

- ¼ cup heavy whipping cream

- 90% dark chocolate, shaved for garnish

Directions:

Beat together the cream cheese until creamy and smooth using a handheld mixer in a medium mixing bowl. Slowly mix in the cocoa powder. Beat in the avocado and mix until creamy smooth, approximately 5 minutes.

Add the vanilla extract and sweetener and beat again until smooth, approximately 1-2 minutes.

In a separate mixing bowl, whip the heavy cream until stiff peaks form.

Place the whipped cream in the chocolate mixture and gently fold until it's incorporated.

Place the chocolate mousse in a piping bag and pipe into desired containers. Garnish with dark chocolate shavings.

41. LOW-CARB TACOS

Prep time: 30 minutes

Cook time: 30 minutes

Total time: 1 hour

Ingredients:

Cheese Taco Shells:

- 2 cups cheddar cheese, shredded

Taco Meat:

- 1 lb ground beef
- 1 tbsp chili powder
- 2 tsp cumin
- 1 tsp onion powder
- 1/2 tsp garlic powder
- 1/4 tsp salt
- 1/4 cup water
- Toppings for taco: Sour cream, avocado, cheese, lettuce, etc.

Directions:

Preheat oven to 350F.

On a baking sheet lined with parchment paper or a silicone mat place 1/4 cup piles of cheese 2 inches apart. Press the cheese down lightly so it makes one layer.

Place baking sheet in the oven and bake for 5-7 minutes or until the edges of the cheese are brown.

Let the cheese cool for 2-3 minutes then lift it up and place it over the handle of a spoon or other utensil that is balanced on two cups.

Let cheese cool completely then remove.

While you continue to bake your cheese taco shells place the ground beef in a skillet over medium high heat cooking until it is completely cooked through.

Drain the grease from the meat and then add the cumin, chili powder, onion, powder, garlic powder, and salt. Pour water into skillet and stir everything around mixing it together.

Simmer for 5 minutes or until liquid has cooked away.

Add meat to taco shells and top with your favorite taco toppings.

42. ALFREDO RECIPE

Total time: 15 minutes

Ingredients:

- 1 small head of cauliflower, chopped (about 3 heaping cups)
- 2 tbsp olive oil
- 2 cloves garlic, smashed and minced
- 2 tsp pine nuts
- 2¼ cup almond milk
- 2 tsp of each: salt, pepper, oregano, and basil
- juice of half a lemon
- ¼ cup plus 1 tbsp nutritional yeast

Directions:

In a medium-sized pot, cook the olive oil, garlic and pine nuts over medium heat for 3–4 minutes, or until garlic is golden brown.

Add in the almond milk and bring to a boil.

Reduce heat to medium and add the cauliflower and spices and cook until cauliflower is soft (about 8 minutes).

Transfer to a high-powered blender and add in the lemon juice and nutritional yeast and blend on high until smooth.

Add over your favorite gluten-free pasta or zoodles and top with fresh basil.

43. LOW-CARB BLUEBERRY MUFFINS

Ingredients:

- ½ stick (2 oz) butter, very soft
- 4 tbsp (2 oz) cream cheese, very soft
- 1/2 tsp vanilla
- ½ cup coconut flour
- ¼ cup Swerve Granulated
- 1 tsp baking powder
- 1/4 tsp salt
- 1/16 tsp cinnamon
- 1/8 tsp xanthan gum
- 3 large eggs
- 1/4 cup heavy cream
- 1/3 cup fresh blueberries
- 2 tsp Swerve Granulated

Directions:

Preheat oven to 350° . Position oven rack to the lower third of the oven. Line a 6-cup muffin tin with paper liners. Add the dry ingredients together in a smaller bowl and whisk together to combine and break up any lumps.

In a medium bowl, cream the butter, cream cheese, and vanilla together until light and fluffy. Add 1 egg and beat into the butter mixture until the mixture is light and fluffy (it may break or separate, it's okay). Add 1/3 of the dry ingredients and mix until completely incorporated, making sure to keep that light, fluffy texture. Keep in mind that we want a light and fluffy – almost mousse-like texture throughout this process.

Add another egg and beat until fully combined and the batter is fluffy. Add half of the remaining dry ingredients, beating again. Add the last egg, beating until fully incorporated, followed by the last of the dry ingredients. Finish by adding the heavy cream, once again, beating until the batter is thick, but still light and fluffy.Fold in the blueberries.

Spoon the thick batter into a plastic zip-loc bag and snip off a corner, producing about a 3/4 inch hole. Place the snipped corner into a muffin liner and squeeze the batter into a fat, rounded mound, filling the muffin liner about 3/4 full. Repeat for each muffin liner, adding any remaining batter to those that need a little more. Knock down any peaks with your finger. Sprinkle about ¼ teaspoon of Swerve granulated over the top of each muffin to help prevent burning and to give the muffins a nice look.

Place the muffins into the oven. Turn the oven up to 400° degrees for 5 minutes. Then, turn the oven back to 350° and bake the blueberry muffins for about 25 minutes more. They're ready when they feel firm when lightly pressed with a finger, but still sound a little moist. Remove from the oven and let cool five minutes before gently removing from the pan and placing on a cooling rack.

44. KETO BEEF WITH BROCCOLI

Prep time: 15 minutes

Cook time: 10 minutes

Total time: 25 minutes

Ingredients:

- 1 lb beef (sirloin, skirt steak, boneless short ribs...etc.)
- 1 to 2 heads broccoli, break into florets
- 2 cloves garlic, minced
- 2 pieces thin sliced ginger, finely chopped
- Ghee or cooking fat of your choice

Beef marinade:

- 2 tbsp coconut aminos
- 1/2 tsp coarse sea salt
- 1 tbsp sesame oil
- 1/4 tsp black pepper
- 1 tsp arrowroot/sweet potato powder
- 1/4 tsp baking soda Baking soda is whole 30 friendly. See notes section.

Sauce combo:

- 2 tbsp coconut aminos
- 1 tbsp red boat fish sauce
- 2 tsp sesame oil
- 1/4 tsp black pepper

Directions:

Slice beef into about ¼ inch thin. Marinate thin sliced beef with ingredients under "beef marinade". Mix well. Place broccoli florets in a microwave safe container. Add 1-2 tablespoons water. Loosely covered with a lid or wet paper towel and microwave for 2 minutes. Cook until broccoli is tender but still crunchy. Set aside.

Heat a wok over medium heat with 1 ½ tablespoons ghee. When hot, lower the heat to medium, add garlic and ginger.Season with a small pinch of salt and stir-fry until fragrant (about 10 seconds).

Turn up the heat to medium-high, add marinated beef. Spread beef evenly over the bottom of the saute pan and cook until the edge of the beef is slightly darkened and crispy. Do the same thing for flip slide - about ¾ way cooked through with slightly charred and crispy surface.

Add "Sauce Combo". Stir-fry about 1 minute. Add broccoli. Stir-fry another 30 seconds. Toss everything to combine.

45. EASY CROCKPOT CHICKEN STEW

Prep time: 5 minutes

Cook time: 2 hours

Total time: 2 hours 5 minutes

Ingredients:

- 2 cups chicken stock
- 2 medium carrots (1/2 cup), peeled and finely diced
- 2 celery sticks (1 cup), diced
- ½ onion (1/2 cup), diced
- 28 oz skinless and deboned chicken thighs diced into 1" pieces
- 1 spring fresh rosemary or ½ tsp dried rosemary
- 3 garlic cloves, minced
- ¼ tsp dried thyme
- ½ tsp dried oregano
- 1 cup fresh spinach
- ½ cup heavy cream
- salt and pepper, to taste

- xantham gum, to desired thickness, starting at ⅛ tsp

Directions:

Place the chicken stock, carrots, celery, onion, chicken thighs, rosemary, garlic, thyme, and oregano into a 3-quart crockpot or larger. Cook on high for 2 hours or on low for 4 hours.

Add salt and pepper, to taste.

Stir in spinach and heavy cream.

Sprinkle and thicken with xantham gum to desired thickness starting at ⅛th teaspoon. Continue to whisk until mix and cook for another 10 minutes.

46. KETO OATMEAL

Prep time: 2 minutes

Total time: 12 hours 2 minutes

You can substitute heavy whipping cream, coconut milk, and almond into any recipe. Generally you will need 75% as much almond milk as you need coconut milk or heavy cream. It's recommended to use chia seeds whenever almond milk is used to create a thicker consistency.

Ingredients:

Pumpkin Pie:

- 3 tbsp hemp hearts
- 1 tbsp 100% pumpkin puree
- 1/2 tsp pumpkin pie spice
- 1 tsp chia aeeds
- 2 drops liquid Stevia
- 3 tbsp unsweetened almond milk

Almond Joy:

- 3 tbsp hemp hearts
- 1/2 tbsp chopped almonds
- 1/2 tbsp Lily's Chocolate Chips
- 1/2 tbsp unsweetened shredded coconut
- 1/4 cup coconut milk
- 1 drop liquid Stevia

Double Chocolate:

- 3 tbsp hemp hearts
- 1 tbsp unsweetened cocoa powder
- 1/2 tbsp Lily's Chocolate Chips
- 1/4 tsp pink salt
- 1/4 cup heavy whipping cream
- 1 tsp chia seeds
- 2 drops liquid Stevia

Maple Walnut:

- 3 tbsp hemp hearts
- 1 tbsp walnuts, chopped
- 1/2 tbsp sugar-free maple syrup

- 1/2 tsp ground cinnamon
- 3 tbsp unsweetened almond milk
- 1 tsp chia seeds

Peanut Butter:

- 3 tbsp hemp hearts
- 1 tbsp peanut butter
- 1 tsp chia seeds
- 1 drop liquid Stevia
- 3 tbsp unsweetened almond milk

Broats:

- 3 tbsp hemp hearts
- 1 tbsp protein powder
- 1 tsp chia seeds
- 1/4 cup heavy whipping cream

Turmeric-Vanilla:

- 3 tbsp hemp hearts
- 1/4 cup coconut milk
- 1 tsp chia seeds

- 1/2 tsp turmeric powder

- 1/2 tsp vanilla extract

- 2 drops liquid Stevia

Directions:

Add all ingredients to a bowl or mason jar. Mix together thoroughly.

Place in the refrigerator overnight, or a minimum of 4 hours. Open the next day and enjoy!

47. LEMON THYME CHICKEN

Ingredients:

- 2 lb grass-fed beef or pork

- 1 1/2 tsp sea salt

- 1 tsp ground black pepper

- 2 large pastured eggs

- 1 medium onion, peeled and finely chopped

- 2 cups mushrooms (any kind will do), finely chopped

- 1/2 cup finely chopped OR grated carrots

- 2 loosely-packed cups of spinach, finely chopped

- 1 tsp dry thyme

- 3 cloves of garlic, peeled and minced

- 1 1/2 tbsp Dijon mustard

Directions:

Preheat your oven to 350 degrees F.

In a large bowl combine all of the ingredients. Using freshly washed hands, mix the ingredients until everything is blended together evenly.

Portion out the meat mixture evenly between a 12-hole muffin tin.

Bake for 25-30 minutes or until meat is cooked.

Enjoy warm with cauliflower rice, a salad, or side of choice.

Freeze leftovers or store in fridge for up to 5 days.

48. KETO PANCAKES

Total time: 20 minutes

Ingredients:

- ½ cup plus 1 tbsp almond flour
- ½ cup grass-fed cream cheese
- 4 eggs
- ½ tsp cinnamon
- 1 tbsp butter or avocado oil, for frying

Directions:

Mix all ingredients in a blender.

In a frying pan, over medium heat, add in the butter or oil.

Pour in 2–3 tablespoons of batter per pancake and turn over once the center begins to bubble (usually takes about 3–4 minutes).

Top with butter and cinnamon

49. KETO CHOCOLATE CHIA PUDDING

Ingredients:

- 1 (13.5 oz) can full-fat coconut milk, blended
- 1 cup water
- 2 tbsp cacao powder
- ⅛ tsp vanilla stevia
- ⅛ tsp Celtic sea salt
- ¼ cup chia seeds

Directions:

In a vitamix, combine coconut milk, water, cacao powder, stevia, and salt.

Blend until smooth.

Transfer mixture to a one quart mason jar.

Add chia seeds and shake well.

Refrigerate overnight to let chia seeds soften and absorb liquid.

Notes: For this recipe, it's important to blend the coconut milk in a high-powered blender. This way you'll have a smooth and creamy pudding, rather than one with little lumps of coconut milk in it.

50. CHEESY GARLIC CREAMED SPINACH

Total time: 5 - 10 minutes

Ingredients:

- 3 tbsp butter
- 4 cloves garlic, minced
- 2 lb fresh spinach leaves
- sea salt and black pepper, to taste
- 1 cup heavy cream
- 1/4 cup grated Parmesan cheese
- 1/4 cup shredded mozzarella cheese
- 1/4 cup goat cheese

Directions:

In a large sauté pan over medium heat, melt the butter. Add the garlic and sauté for 1 minute, being careful not to burn it.

Add the spinach. Season with sea salt and black pepper to taste.Sauté until the spinach is wilted. Remove the spinach from the pan and let it drain.

You may need to press it in a colander to remove all of the excess moisture.

To the same pan, add the heavy cream, Parmesan, mozzarella and goat cheeses. Lower the heat to low and allow the sauce to thicken, 5 to 10 minutes. Add the wilted spinach back to the pan and toss until evenly coated in the creamy cheese sauce.

51. CHICKEN IN WHITE SAUCE

Prep time: 10 minutes

Cook time: 40 minutes

Total time: 50 minutes

Ingredients:

- 4 chicken breasts, medium sized
- 1 cup coconut cream
- 1 cup white wine
- 300 g mushrooms
- 300 g green beans, halved
- 2 tsp Dijon mustard
- 4 cloves garlic
- ¼ cup olive oil
- 1 tsp fresh thyme, chopped
- 1 tsp salt
- 1 tsp pepper

Directions:

Preheat the oven to 355F (180C).

Heat a frying pan to medium heat with half the amount of olive oil required for the recipe, add the chicken breasts and cook each side for 2 minutes.

Place the chicken on baking tray lined with baking paper. Cook for 15 minutes.

Meanwhile, in the same frying pan, slice the mushrooms and slightly brown them using the reaining olive oil and garlic.

Add the beans, coconut cream, white wine, dijon mustard, thyme, salt and pepper. Mix around in the pan and reduce to a simmer. The sauce should be quite watery to start with, and will reduce to a lovely creamy sauce.

Once the chicken has reached 15 minutes, remove from the oven. Plate the chicken and cover with sauce, mushrooms, and beans.

52. GUILTLESS GARLIC PARMESAN WINGS

Total time: 35 minutes

Ingredients:

- 12 chicken wings
- 1½ tbsp avocado oil
- 1 tbsp garlic powder
- ½ cup parmesan, grated
- ½ cup pecorino romano, grated
- 1 tsp salt
- 1 tsp pepper

Directions:

Preheat oven to 350 F.

Line a baking sheet with parchment and set aside.

Mix spices and cheeses in a bowl.

Coat the wings in oil.

Dip wings in mixture.

Bake for 30 minutes.

53. Eggplant Rollatini Recipe

Total time: 1 hour

Ingredients:

- 2 large eggplants, sliced lengthwise
- ½ tsp sea salt
- ½ tsp black pepper
- 1–1½ cups marinara sauce
- 2 large eggs
- 3 cups spinach
- 1 package goat feta (4 oz)
- 1 tsp dried oregano
- 1 tsp parsley
- 1 tsp dried basil
- 2 cups pecorino romano, grated
- 1 cup raw sheep cheese, grated

Directions:

Preheat oven to 450 F.

While your oven is heating up, cut the ends off of the two eggplants and then slice lengthwise.

Place the eggplant slices on a baking sheet lined with parchment paper and sprinkle with salt and pepper.

Bake for 12–15 minutes, remove and allow to cool.

Reduce heat to 400 F.

In a medium bowl, mix the eggs, goat cheese, spinach, oregano, parsley, basil, 1 cup pecorino romano, ½ cup raw sheep cheese, salt and pepper, mixing until well combined.

In a 9x13 baking dish, add ¾ cup marinara.

Place ¼ cup cheese mixture onto one end of the sliced eggplant, then roll it up and transfer to baking dish, continuing until baking dish is full.

Cover with remaining marinara and cheese.

Bake for 25 minutes and allow to cool for 10 minutes before serving.

54. KETO SMOOTHIE RECIPE WITH AVOCADO, CHIA SEEDS & CACAO

Total time: 15 minutes

Ingredients:

- 1–1¼ cups full-fat coconut milk
- ½ frozen avocado
- 1 tbsp nut butter of choice
- 1 tbsp chia seeds, soaked in 3 tablespoons of water for 10 minutes
- 2 tsp cacao nibs, cacao powder or cocoa powder or 1 scoop of chocolate protein powder made from bone broth
- 1 tbsp coconut oil
- ice (optional)

For topping:

- cacao nibs and cinnamon
- ¼ cup water, if needed

Directions:

Add ingredients into a high-powered blender, processing until well-combined.

Top with cacao nibs and cinnamon.

55. LOW-CARB CAULIFLOWER POT PIES

Prep time: 15 minutes

Cook time: 25 minutes

Total time: 40 minutes

Ingredients:

Cauliflower Base:

- 1 medium head cauliflower (4-5 cups cauliflower rice)
- 1/4 cup shredded parmesan cheese
- 1 egg
- pinch of salt and pepper

Pot Pie Filling:

- 1/2 onion, diced
- 1 1/2 cups chicken broth
- 1/4 cup almond milk, unsweetened
- 1 cup frozen mixed vegetables
- 8 oz cooked chicken, diced

- 1 tbsp onion powder

- 1/2 tsp salt

- 1/2 tsp black pepper

- 2 tbs cornstarch, plus 1/4 cup water

Instructions:

Preheat oven to 400° F. Add the cauliflower to the bowl of a food processor and pulse until you achieve a rice-like consistency. Transfer cauliflower "rice" to a bowl and microwave for 5 minutes. Set aside and allow cauliflower to cool for approx 10 minutes.

Add the cauliflower rice to a cheesecloth and squeeze out as much of the juice from the cauliflower as possible. If you don't, the bases may end up soggy (the key here is to really get as much of that juice out as you can). Once you have done a round with the cheesecloth. Repeat with another dry cheesecloth to ensure you have removed a majority of the liquid.

Add the dried cauliflower rice to a bowl with the egg, parmesan cheese, salt and pepper. Using your hands, combine all of the ingredients thoroughly. Spray a large muffin pan or 4 ramekins and gently press the cauliflower mixture to the sides, creating a cauliflower bowl. Bake for 20-25 minutes or until the centers are dry and the edges are golden brown.

While the cauliflower bases are in the oven, spray a medium saucepan with cooking spray and saute the diced onion on high heat until slightly tender. Reduce heat to medium and add the chicken broth, almond milk, mixed vegetables, onion powder, salt and black pepper. Stir and cover for approx 5-8 minutes or until frozen vegetables are soft.

Mix the cornstarch with the water to make a slurry and add to the sauce with the cooked chicken. Stir in the cornstarch mixture and increase heat to high and cook until sauce begins to boil. Remove from heat.

Fill each cauliflower base with the pot pie filling and serve.

56. JALAPENO POPPERS

Total time: 25 minutes

Ingredients:

- 10–12 jalapeno peppers, stemmed removed, sliced in ½ length-wise and seeds removed
- 1 package turkey bacon (optional*)
- ½-1 cup goat feta
- ½-1 cup shredded goat cheese
- ½ tsp cumin
- ½ tsp chili powder
- ½ tsp smoked paprika
- ½ tsp oregano
- salt and pepper to taste

Directions:

Preheat oven to 350 F.

Line a baking sheet, or two, with parchment paper and set aside.

In a medium-sized bowl add everything except the jalapeños and turkey bacon, mixing until well-combined.

Using your hands, fill each halved jalapeño with the cheese mixture.

Wrap jalapeno with turkey bacon and place on baking sheet.

Bake for 20 minutes.

Pair with our Avocado Ranch Dressing.

57. KETO LOW-CARB GRANOLA CEREAL

Prep time: 10 minutes

Cook time: 15 minutes

Total time: 25 minutes

Ingredients:

- 1 cup almonds

- 1 cup hazelnuts

- 1 cup pecans

- 1/3 cup pumpkin seeds

- 1/3 cup sunflower seeds

- 6 tbsp Erythritol

- 1/2 cup golden flaxseed meal

- 1 large egg white

- 1/4 cup butter (measured solid, then melted; can use coconut oil or ghee for dairy-free)

- 1 tsp vanilla extract

Directions:

Preheat oven to 325° F. Line a large baking sheet, or two small ones, with parchment paper.

Pulse almonds and hazelnuts in a food processor intermittently, until most of the nuts are in chopped into large pieces (about 1/4 to 1/2 of the full size of the nuts).

Add the pecans. Pulse again, stopping when the pecans are in large pieces (pecans are added later since they are softer).

Add the pumpkin seeds, sunflower seeds, erythritol, and golden flaxseed meal. Pulse just until everything is mixed well. Don't over-process! You want to have plenty of nut pieces remaining, and most of the seeds should be intact.

Add the egg white to the food processor. Whisk together the melted butter and vanilla extract in a small bowl, and evenly pour that in, too.

Pulse a couple times, mix a little from the bottom toward the top with a spatula, then pulse a couple times again. Repeat as needed until everything is coated evenly. Again, avoid over-processing. At the end of this step, you'll have a combination of coarse meal and nut pieces, and everything should be a little damp from the egg white and butter.

Transfer the nut mixture to the prepared baking sheet in a uniform layer, pressing together into a thin rectangle (about 1/4 to 1/3 in (.6-.8 cm) thick). Bake for 15-18 minutes, until lightly browned, especially at the edges.

Cool completely before breaking apart into pieces (the granola will be soft when you remove it from the oven, but will crisp up as it cools).

58. KETO ZUCCHINI BREAD WITH WALNUTS

Ingredients:

- 3 large eggs
- ½ cup olive oil
- 1 tsp vanilla extract
- 2 ½ cups almond flour
- 1 ½ cups erythritol
- ½ tsp salt
- 1 ½ tsp baking powder
- ½ tsp nutmeg
- 1 tsp ground cinnamon
- ¼ tsp ground ginger
- 1 cup grated zucchini
- ½ cup chopped walnuts

Directions:

Preheat oven to 350°F. Whisk together the eggs, oil, and vanilla extract. Set to the side.

In another bowl, mix together the almond flour, erythritol, salt, baking powder, nutmeg, cinnamon, and ginger. Set to the side.

Using a cheesecloth or paper towel, take the zucchini and squeeze out the excess water.

Then, whisk the zucchini into the bowl with the eggs.

Slowly add the dry ingredients into the egg mixture using a hand mixer until fully blended.

Lightly spray a 9×5 loaf pan, and spoon in the zucchini bread mixture.

Then, spoon in the chopped walnuts on top of the zucchini bread. Press walnuts into the batter using a spatula.

Bake for 60-70 minutes at 350°F or until the walnuts on top look browned.

59. KETO WALNUT BREAD

Ingredients:

- 3 large eggs
- ½ cup olive oil
- 1 tsp vanilla extract
- 2 1/2 cups almond flour
- 1 1/2 cups erythritol
- ½ tsp salt
- 1 1/2 tsp baking powder
- ½ tsp nutmeg
- 1 tsp ground cinnamon
- ¼ tsp ground ginger
- 1 cup grated zucchini
- ½ cup chopped walnuts

Directions:

Preheat oven to 350°F. Whisk together the eggs, oil, and vanilla extract. Set to the side.

In another bowl, mix together the almond flour, erythritol, salt, baking powder, nutmeg, cinnamon, and ginger. Set to the side.

Using a cheesecloth or paper towel, take the zucchini and squeeze out the excess water.

Then, whisk the zucchini into the bowl with the eggs.

Slowly add the dry ingredients into the egg mixture using a hand mixer until fully blended.

Lightly spray a 9x5 loaf pan, and spoon in the zucchini bread mixture.

Then, spoon in the chopped walnuts on top of the zucchini bread. Press walnuts into the batter using a spatula.

Bake for 60-70 minutes at 350°F or until the walnuts on top look browned.

60. LOW-CARB TORTILLA CHIPS

Prep time: 10 minutes

Cook time: 10 minutes

Total time: 20 minutes

Ingredients:

- 2 cups almond flour
- 1/2 tsp chili powder
- 1/2 tsp garlic powder
- 1/2 tsp cumin
- 1/4 tsp paprika
- 1/4 tsp sea salt
- 1 large egg, beaten
- 1/2 cup mozzarella cheese, shredded

Directions:

Preheat the oven to 350° F . Line a baking sheet with parchment paper.

In a large bowl, mix together the almond flour and spices.

Add the egg and mix using a hand mixer, until a crumbly dough forms.

In a small bowl, microwave the mozzarella until it's melted and easy to stir (alternatively, you can melt it using a double broiler on the stove). Add to the dough mixture and knead/squeeze with your hands until well incorporated. If it stops incorporating before it's fully mixed, you can reheat it for 15-20 seconds again before kneading more.

Place the dough between two large pieces of parchment paper. Use a rolling pin to roll out very thin, about 1/16 in (2 mm) thick.

Cut the dough into triangles and arranged on the parchment lined baking sheet. Bake for 8-12 minutes, until golden and firm. The chips may release some sizzling oil on the top - just pat dry with a paper towel. They will crisp up as they cool.

61. PUMPKIN SPICE KETO FAT BOMB RECIPE

Prep time: 10 minutes

Ingredients:

- 1/2 cup coconut oil

- 3/4 cup pumpkin puree

- 1/3 cup golden flax

- 1 tsp cinnamon or I used 2 drops cinnamon bark vitality essential oil

- 1/2 tsp nutmeg

- 1/4 tsp sea salt

- 1/4 cup confectioner's Swerve or 1/3 tsp stevia or to taste

Directions:

Mix all the ingredients in a bowl and place in the freezer for 30 minutes. Roll into balls and place on a plate. Let the balls sit in the refrigerator for 1 hours before eating. Keeps for a week or longer in the freezer.

62. EASY CHEESY ZUCCHINI GRATIN

Ingredients:

- 4 cups sliced raw zucchini
- 1 small onion, peeled and sliced thin
- salt and pepper to taste
- 1 1/2 cups shredded pepper jack cheese
- 2 tbsp butter
- 1/2 tsp garlic powder
- 1/2 cup heavy whipping cream

Instructions:

Preheat oven to 375° F.

Grease a 9×9 or equivalent oven-proof pan.

Overlap 1/3 of the zucchini and onion slices in the pan, then season with salt and pepper and sprinkle with 1/2 cup of shredded cheese.

Repeat two more times until you have three layers and have used up all of the zucchini, onions, and shredded cheese.

Combine the garlic powder, butter, and heavy cream in a microwave safe dish.

Heat for one minute or until the butter has melted. Stir.

Gently pour the butter and cream mixture over the zucchini layers.

Bake at 375° F for about 45 minutes, or until the liquid has thickened and the top is golden brown.

Serve warm.

63. KETO SNACKS

Total time: 25 minutes

Ingredients:

- 4–6 eggs
- 1 avocado
- ¼ tsp sea salt
- ¼ tsp pepper
- ¼ tsp garlic
- ¼ tsp chili powder
- ¼ tsp cumin
- ¼ tsp smoked paprika, optional*
- 2 tbsp cilantro

Directions:

In a medium pot, add eggs and cover with water until fully submerged.

Bring to a boil, then remove from heat and cover for 12–13 minutes.

Fill a large bowl with ice water and, using a slotted spoon, gently place eggs in the bowl, allowing eggs to chill for 5 minutes.

Remove outer casing from eggs and slice in half lengthwise, removing the yolk.

Add the yolk, along with the avocado and spices to a bowl, mixing together until well combined.

Add the mixture to the egg halves.

Drizzle with lime juice and top with cilantro.

64. BLACKBERRY-NUT FAT BOMBS

Ingredients:

- 2 oz macadamia nuts, crushed
- 4 oz neufchatel cheese (cream cheese)
- 1 cup blackberries
- 3 tbsp mascarpone cheese
- 1 cup coconut oil
- 1 cup coconut butter
- 1/2 tsp vanilla extract
- 1/2 tsp lemon juice
- stevia to taste

Directions:

Crush the macadamia nuts and press into the bottom of a baking dish or mold. Bake 5 to 7 minutes at 325 F, or until golden brown.

Remove from the oven and allow to cool slightly.

Spread a layer of softened cream cheese over the nut "crust."

In a bowl, mix together blackberries, mascarpone cheese, coconut oil, coconut butter, vanilla, lemon juice and sweetener (optional) until smooth.

Pour mixture over the cream cheese layer. Freeze for 30 minutes to an hour. Remove and store in the fridge.

65. BUFFALO KETO CHICKEN TENDERS

Prep time: 10 minutes

Cook time: 30 minutes

Total time: 40 minutes

Ingredients:

- 1 lb chicken breast tenders
- 1 cup almond flour
- 1 large egg
- 1 tbsp heavy whipping cream
- 6 oz Buffalo sauce
- salt & pepper

Instructions:

Preheat oven to 350°.

Season chicken tenders with salt and pepper. Season the almond flour generously with salt and pepper.

Beat 1 egg together with 1 tablespoon of heavy cream.

Dip each tender first in the egg wash and then into the seasoned almond flour. We like to place the tenders in a Tupperware container with the almond flour and shake to coat. A Ziploc bag also works well.

Place tenders on a lightly greased baking sheet. Bake for 30 minutes. If they are not as crispy as you would like you can additionally broil them for 2-3 minutes.

Allow tenders to cool for 5 minutes and then place them in a tupperware container, add the buffalo sauce and shake to coat. Gently shaking is best to prevent the batter from falling off.

66. COCONUT KETO MILK

Prep time: 2 minutes

Cook time: 3 minutes

Total time: 5 minutes

Ingredients:

- ½ cup filtered water
- ½ cup coconut milk
- 2 tbsp unsalted butter (grass-fed)
- 1 tbsp coconut oil or MCT oil
- 2 tbsp unsweetened cocoa powder
- ¼ tsp vanilla extract
- dash cinnamon
- 1-2 teaspoons Erythritol –(optional)

Directions:

In a medium sized pot (if using hand blender) or a small pot (if using blender), bring water and coconut milk to a boil.

Remove from heat.

Add the rest of the ingredients into the coconut milk and water.

Blend using a hand blender (like the ones for soups) or pour the mixture into a blender and blend till frothy.

67. KETO CHEESE MEATBALLS

Prep time: 10 minutes

Cook time: 10 minutes

Total time: 20 minutes

Ingredients:

- 500 g ground beef
- 100 g cheese, mozzarella works best, but cheddar is fine
- 3 tbsp Parmesan cheese
- 1 tsp garlic Powder
- 1/2 tsp salt
- 1/2 tsp pepper

Directions:

Cut the cheese into cubes (1cm by 1cm).

Mix the dry ingredients with the ground beef.

Wrap the cubes of cheese in the meat (500g should make about 9 balls).

Pan fry the meatballs (cover with a lid to capture the heat all around). Fingers crossed the cheese doesn't spill.

68. COCONUT BOOSTERS RECIPE

Total time: 65 minutes

Ingredients:

- 1 cup coconut oil
- 1/2 cup chia seeds
- 1 tsp vanilla extract
- 1 tbsp honey
- 1/4 cup unsweetened coconut flakes

Directions:

Using a hand mixer, combine all ingredients together in a bowl.

Spoon into muffin cups/muffin tins and freeze for an hour.

Sprinkle with extra coconut flakes if desired.

69. BAKED MEATBALLS RECIPE

Total time: 15 minutes

Ingredients:

- 1 lb beef
- ½ lb of both: lamb and bison
- ⅓ cup raw, smoked goat cheese
- ¼ cup of: fresh parsley, fresh basil and oregano, all finely chopped
- 1-2 tbsp melted coconut oil
- 1 tsp sea salt
- 1 tsp pepper
- 1 tsp onion powder
- 2 eggs
- 1 tbsp cassava flour

Directions:

Preheat oven to 375 F.

Line two baking sheets with parchment paper and set aside.

Add all ingredients to a large bowl and, using your hands, mix until well combined.

Roll into small meatballs and place on baking sheets.

Bake for 12-15 minutes or until internal temperature reaches 165 F.

70. GOAT CHEESE & ARTICHOKE DIP RECIPE

Total time: 5 minutes

Ingredients:

- 14-oz can artichoke hearts, drained
- 1 lb chévre goat cheese
- 2 tbsp olive oil
- 2 tsp lemon juice
- 1 garlic clove, minced
- ½ cup pecorino romano, grated
- 1 tbsp parsley
- 1 tsp chives
- ½ tbsp basil
- ½ tsp sea salt
- ½ tsp black pepper
- Dash of cayenne pepper (optional)

Directions:

In a food processor, mix all ingredients except the pecorino romano until well incorporated and creamy.

Top with freshly-grated pecorino romano.

71. LOW-CARB INDIAN SAMOSAS

Prep time: 25 minutes

Cook time: 17 minutes

Total time: 37 minutes

Ingredients:

- 1 tbsp butter preferably grass-fed
- 6 oz cauliflower finely chopped
- 1 medium onion, about 4 oz
- 3/4 tsp salt (or to taste)
- 1 tbsp fresh ginger root, minced
- 1/2 tsp coriander ground
- 1 tsp garam masala ground
- 1 tsp cumin ground
- 1/4 tsp cumin seeds whole
- 1/8-1/4 tsp red chili flakes
- 1/4 cup fresh cilantro chopped

Dough:

- 3/4 cup super-fine almond flour

- 1/4 tsp cumin

- 1/2 tsp salt

- 8 oz part-skim mozzarella cheese, finely shredded

Directions:

For the filling:

Preheat a large skillet over medium heat. Add butter. When butter has melted and stopped foaming, add the cauliflower and onions.

Sprinkle the salt over the vegetables.Cook, stirring occasionally, until the edges have started to brown and the vegetables are cooked through.

Stir in ginger root, coriander, garam masala, ground cumin, cumin seeds, and chili flakes. Stir for 1-2 minutes to allow the spices to toast. Turn off the heat.

Stir in the cilantro. Taste and adjust seasoning. Add salt to taste.

Preheat oven to 375° F. Have a rolling pin, 2 pieces of parchment, and a baking sheet available.

For the dough:

Set up a double boiler. I use a large sauce pan with about 1 1/2-2 inches of water in it and a medium mixing bowl that fits on top.

Bring the water in the lower part of the double boiler to a simmer over high heat. Once it is simmering, turn heat to low.

Meanwhile, place the almond flour, cumin, salt, and mozzarella in the top part of the double boiler. Stir together.

Place the bowl containing the almond flour mixture over the simmering water. Be careful not to burn yourself with the hot bowl or with steam escaping. I use a silicone mitten to hold the bowl.

Stirring the mixture constantly, heat until the mozzarella cheese melts and the mixture forms a dough.

Turn the dough out onto one of the pieces of parchment and knead a few times to equally distribute the ingredients. Shape the dough into a thick rectangle and cover with the second sheet of parchment. Roll dough into a rectangle about 8 inches wide by 16 inches long.

Cut the dough rectangle in half lengthwise, then in half cross-wise. Then cut each of the four sections in half crosswise to form 8 four-inch squares.

To assemble:

Spoon the filling onto the center of each square, dividing it equally among the squares. Fold the squares on the diagonal to form triangles and pinch the edges closed. Place one of the pieces of parchment used to roll out the dough onto a baking sheet, then place the samosas on the sheet.

Make fork holes in each samosa to provide a place for steam to release. Bake for 14-17 minutes or until golden-brown.

72.   CHOCOLATE AVOCADO PUDDING

Total time: 5 minutes

Ingredients:

- 1/4 cup unsweetened cocoa powder
- 1 medium avocado
- 10 drops liquid Stevia
- 1/2 tsp vanilla extract
- 1 tsp pink salt

Directions:

Remove the pit from the avocado and place in a mixing bowl.

Add cocoa powder, stevia, and vanilla extract and mix with a fork until a pudding is formed. You can gently use a hand mixer also, but a fork does the job.

Top with pink sea salt.

73. LOADED HASSELBACK ZUCCHINI

Prep time: 10 minutes

Cook time: 15 minutes

Total time: 25 minutes

Ingredients:

- 3 medium zucchini squash
- about 6-8 oz of your favorite cheese
- 3-4 tbsp sour cream
- 3 slices of crumbled cooked bacon
- 2-3 tbsp chopped green onion
- salt and pepper, to taste

Notes: For this recipe you can use sliced cheese (pre-sliced or sliced fresh off the block) or shredded cheese. Both work great, but I find using slices the easiest. I cut my slices off the block, then cut each slice in half. You can even skip the stuffing portion altogether and whisk together a simple nacho-style cheddar cheese sauce to pour over each zucchini. Anything goes when it comes to cheese.

Directions:

Preheat oven to 425° F.

Wash and dry zucchini, and slice off the ends.

Line up a chopstick on both sides of the squash and slice until you hit the stick.

Start at one end and keep slicing into discs (granted - connected discs since we don't want to cut all the way through the squash) until you've reached the other end. Repeat for remaining squash.

Resist the urge to play the zucchini accordion-style when you're done.

Slice each zucchini in half so you have 6 mini hasselbacks.

Line a baking sheet with foil, then arrange your zukes on top.

Next, stuff cheese between each tasty little zucchini disc.

Season with salt and pepper if desired and top with another sheet of foil.

Pinch along the sides to make a foil pouch.

The foil pouch will not only help the zucchini cook quicker by steaming the squash, but will also keep the cheese melty and prevent it from browning.

Bake at 425° F for 15-20 minutes.

Allow to rest/steam covered in foil for an additional 5.

Top with sour cream, bacon, and green onion and dig in.

74.   GUILTLESS GARLIC PARMESAN WINGS

Total time: 35 minutes

Ingredients:

- 12 chicken wings
- 1½ tbsp avocado oil
- 1 tbsp garlic powder
- ½ cup parmesan, grated
- ½ cup pecorino romano, grated
- 1 tsp salt

1 tsp pepper

D● irections:

Preheat oven to 350 F.

Line a baking sheet with parchment and set aside.

Mix spices and cheeses in a bowl.

Coat the wings in oil.

Dip wings in mixture.

Bake for 30 minutes.

75. EGGPLANT ROLLATINI RECIPE

Total time: 1 hour

Ingredients:

- 2 large eggplants, sliced lengthwise
- ½ tsp sea salt
- ½ tsp black pepper
- 1–1½ cups marinara sauce
- 2 large eggs
- 3 cups spinach
- 1 package goat feta (4 oz)
- 1 tsp dried oregano
- 1 tsp parsley
- 1 tsp dried basil
- 2 cups pecorino romano, grated
- 1 cup raw sheep cheese, grated

Directions:

Preheat oven to 450 F.

While the oven is heating up, cut the ends off of the two eggplants and then slice lengthwise.

Place the eggplant slices on a baking sheet lined with parchment paper and sprinkle with salt and pepper.

Bake for 12–15 minutes, remove and allow to cool.

Reduce heat to 400 F.

In a medium bowl, mix the eggs, goat cheese, spinach, oregano, parsley, basil, 1 cup pecorino romano, ½ cup raw sheep cheese, salt and pepper, mixing until well combined.

In a 9x13 baking dish, add ¾ cup marinara.

Place ¼ cup cheese mixture onto one end of the sliced eggplant, then roll it up and transfer to baking dish, continuing until baking dish is full.

Cover with remaining marinara and cheese.

Bake for 25 minutes and allow to cool for 10 minutes before serving

76. MEATBALLS

Prep time: 15 minutes

Cook time: 15 minutes

Total time: 30 minutes

Ingredients:

- 1/4 cup grated Parmesan cheese
- 1/4 cup golden flaxseed meal
- 1 tbsp Italian seasoning
- 3/4 tsp sea salt
- 1/2 tsp black pepper
- 1/4 cup unsweetened coconut milk beverage (or any milk of choice)
- 3 tbsp onion, grated
- 1 large egg
- 3 cloves garlic, minced
- 2 tbsp fresh parsley chopped
- 1 lb ground beef
- 3/4 cup marinara sauce

Directions:

Preheat the oven to 425° F. Line a baking sheet with parchment paper or foil (grease if using foil).

In a large bowl, stir together the grated Parmesan cheese, golden flaxseed meal, Italian seasoning, sea salt, and black pepper.

Whisk in the milk, grated onion, egg, garlic, and fresh parsley. Let the mixture sit for a couple of minutes.

Mix in the ground beef using your hands, until just incorporated (don't over-mix to avoid tough meatballs).

Form the mixture into 1-inch balls and place on the lined baking sheet (a small cookie scoop works well for this. If using your hands, use a gentle touch and don't pack the meatballs too tightly).

Bake for 10-12 minutes, until the meatballs are barely done (if you want them more golden, you can place them under the broiler for a couple of minutes).

Top each meatball with marinara sauce. Return to the oven and bake for 3-5 minutes, until the sauce is

hot and meatballs are cooked through. Garnish with
additional fresh parsley.

182

HOW TO STORE FOOD SAFELY AND PREVENT FOODBORNE ILLNESSES

Some foods are more susceptible to harmful pathogens than others, like milk and dairy products, eggs, beef, pork, lamb, poultry, fish, shellfish, baked potatoes, cooked rice, sprouts, sliced melons, cut melons, untreated garlic, and oil mixtures and many, many more.

Prevention of foodborne illnesses should be a primary focus of every kitchen in America. Each year, millions of people get sick from unsafe foods and over 30% of the suspected cases of foodborne illness happens at home.

Here are the five most common risk factors causing foodborne illnesses as identified by the CDC (Centers for Disease Control):

1. Purchasing food from unsafe food sources.

2. Failing to cook food adequately.

3. Holding food at incorrect temperatures.

4. Using contaminated equipment.

5. Practicing poor personal hygiene.

You can help to keep your holiday foods safe by controlling FAT TOM. What is FAT TOM? FAT TOM is the six conditions in which pathogens grow. Taking care of these six conditions helps prevent outbreaks of foodborne illnesses.

F = Food. Pathogens need a source of energy.

A = Acidity. Foods that contain little or no acidity are where pathogens grown best.

T = Temperature. Pathogens grow best in food held between 41°F and 135°F. This is known as the "danger zone."

T = time. Pathogens need time to grow. After four hours, food left in the danger zone will grow a high enough legal of pathogens to make someone sick.

O = Oxygen. Some pathogens need oxygen to grow while some others grow where there is no oxygen.

M = Moisture. Pathogens need moisture in food to grow.

As you can see, these items are easy to follow. Become familiar with these tips and use your new knowledge to keep food safe and thereby help to keep your family and guests safe.

When you are thinking about starting a long-term food storage program, there many things to consider. First off, what are your food storage goals? A common guideline is to start with a three-month supply of foods you normally eat, and then build up a one-year supply of longer-term foods.

What IS long-term food storage? This concept is basically to have a supply of food that can sustain your family for one year in case of a long-lasting emergency situation. These bulk foods tend to have long shelf lives and when combined with a few other ingredients can make a wide variety of meals. Some of the most common foods stored are wheat, oats, rice, legumes, powdered milk, oil, salt, yeast, etc. Basically the staple foods of any diet.

How much should you store? While there are basic food storage calculators out there to help you along the way, they aren't necessarily exactly right for every situation. Here are some do's and don'ts that can help you as you get started with your family's personal plan.

Food Storage Do's:

- DO get a partner to work with you, share ideas, and motivate you.

- DO learn how to actually USE the foods that you are storing.

- DO buy the necessary kitchen appliances to help you use the foods.

- DO include the foods you store as part of your everyday cooking.

- DO be adventurous and try new recipes.

- DO start small and work your way up to a full year supply.

- DO make sure to have an emergency plan in place.

- DO expand your food storage to include other things once you get the basics down.

- DO educate yourself in other aspects of emergency preparedness such as alternative heating/cooking methods.

Food Storage Don'ts:

- DON'T get overwhelmed and just give up completely.

- DON'T store foods that your family hates just because the calculator says to.

- DON'T think that cooking with these foods is fattening and unhealthy.

- DON'T think that using bulk foods and cooking from scratch is really inconvenient.

- DON'T get too crazy about figuring out how to cook without electricity when you are just getting started.

- DON'T buy everything all at once and kill your budget.

- DON'T try to get your family to change their diet completely over night.

- DON'T be too anxious to buy things that you don't wait for good sales.

- DON'T focus too much on long-term items and neglect to store some basic foods you use on a regular basis.

CONCLUSION

Gone is the myth that a keto diet is unappetizing, unpalatable, boring and unappealing! Beautifully-illustrated recipes for 76 different delicious meals are testimony to this

I highly recommend the "Keto Meal Prep for Beginners" because in the world of the Ketogenic diet, it would be hard to match the combined knowledge and experience of the authors.

It is hard to estimate the happiness brought to a family suffering with uncontrollable seizures when the Keto Diet is successful in reducing or eliminating seizures. From watching helplessly as their child slowly deteriorates and slips behind developmentally, to seeing the success of the diet - the child re-emerging with their previously known persona, developmentally progressing, regaining speech and other important milestones is an unimaginable stress replaced with incomparable joy for those involved.

Before coming to the conclusion, other factors need to be considered such as activity levels, type of ketogenic diet, length of ketogenic diet, past eating experience, purpose of ketogeninc diet, individual body type, and response to various eating plans, current physical condition, and quality of food while following the ketogenic diet. As you can see, there are numerous factors that come into play when saying a diet is good or bad.